St Cross College
Recipes and Stories

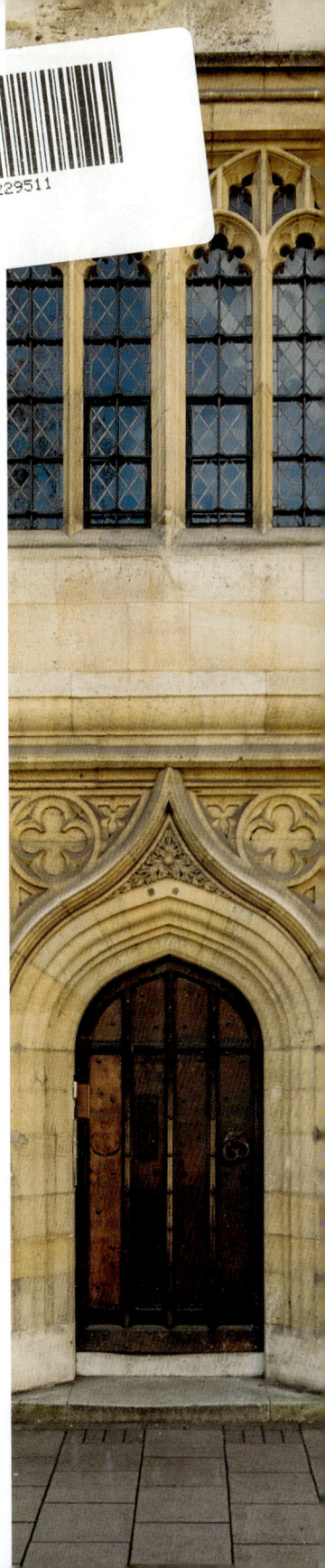

ST CROSS COLLEGE

Recipes and Stories

Edited by
Olena Seminog

Masters and Doctoral Student,
St Cross College, 2010-2016

Contents

Foreword *Carole Souter (Master of St Cross College)* — 6
Preface *Olena Seminog (Editor. Doctoral student, St Cross College)* — 7
Acknowledgements — 9
Useful Information — 10

Sides, Salads and Starters — 11

- Stuffed vine leaves *Israel/Palestine* — 12
- Pourgouri pilaf *Cyprus* — 15
- Pan-fried aubergine *Ukraine* — 16
- Insalata di Rinforzo: Italian Christmas salad *Italy* — 18
- Beetroot salad from the Australian coast *Australia* — 20
- Potato salad *United States* — 22
- Winter root vegetable salad *Ukraine* — 24
- Pumpkin and coconut soup *Fusion* — 26
- Chicken wings braised in coca-cola and soy sauce *China* — 28
- Chinese dumplings *China* — 30
- Smoked salmon and cod mousse parcels *France* — 32
- Seared King scallop (with extras): 50th anniversary dinner *United Kingdom* — 34
- Cock-a-Leekie soup: Burns' night dinner *Scotland* — 36
- Brown Windsor soup *England* — 38

Mains — 39

- Porridge with chia and coconut milk (for Breakfast) *United Kingdom* — 40
- Ukrainian Christmas meal "Kutia" *Ukraine* — 41
- Traditional Ukrainian Varenyky *Ukraine* — 44
- Taboulé *Israel* — 46
- Bibimbap *South Korea* — 48
- Lasagne *Italy* — 51
- Spicy vegetarian chili *United States* — 52
- Upgraded ready-made curry *United Kingdom* — 54
- Curry with lamb and prunes *India* — 56
- Salmon rolls with cream cheese *India* — 58

Nellie Shackelford Saunders' Chesapeake Bay crab cakes *United States*	60
Basque cod with Pil Pil sauce *Basque*	62
Mustard and balsamic chicken *United Kingdom*	64
Braised Greek chicken *Greece*	66
Braised pheasant *United Kingdom*	68
Chilean baked beef empanadas *Chile*	71
Risotto with lambs' kidneys *Italy/India*	74
Punjene Paprike: stuffed peppers *Yugoslavia*	76
Moo gratiem pork with garlic *Thailand*	78
Afelia (Cypriot pork) *Cyprus*	80
Galapagos seafood rice *Ecuador*	82
Loin of venison (with extras): 50th anniversary dinner *United Kingdom*	84
Haggis, neaps and tatties: Burns' night dinner *Scotland*	86
Japanese curry and rice *Japan*	88

Desserts and Drinks   89

Dutch cake with chocolate flakes *The Netherlands*	90
The Oxford graduate students' tiramisu *Italy*	92
Caramel squares *United Kingdom*	94
Oatmeal and yogurt pancakes *United States*	96
Mom's melting shortbread *Canada*	98
Apfel strudel *Germany*	100
Apple Crumble *United Kingdom*	102
Venezuelan rum cake "Bienmesabe" *Venezuela*	104
Chocolate and chestnut log *United Kingdom*	106
Fig and hazelnut frangipane tart: 50th anniversary dinner *United Kingdom*	108
Cranachan: Burns' night dinner *Scotland*	110
Fruit smoothie *Taiwan*	112
Bloody Charles house cocktail *United Kingdom*	114
Eggs 'n' Baker *United Kingdom*	115

50th Anniversary Dinner   116

Burns' Night Dinner   118

Foreword

Before I took up my post as Master of St Cross, in September 2016, I spoke to as many people as I could, and read everything I could find, about the College.

I was puzzled by how many people talked about the College food. Until, that is, I arrived and realised that sharing good food around a common table is central to what St Cross is all about. At lunch time students, Fellows, staff, and Members of Common Room from all over the world – many accompanied by guests from the University and beyond – find themselves a space at one of our three long tables and sit down to talk and eat and make new friendships.

At evening Halls and Special Dinners the menus and food are more formal and worthy of any fine restaurant, but the same egalitarian principles of a community eating together apply. Special days, such as graduations, are made more special by the familiarity of a full Dining Hall, shared with proud parents and friends. And just about any occasion is a good excuse for tea and cakes.

So good food brings people to our tables and Common Rooms, but it is the conversation and friendship that encourages them to linger.

This book is a tangible expression of the affection that so many people feel for St Cross and of the diversity of our College community. With alumni in over 100 countries, it is no surprise that the recipes that follow also come from all over the world. The contributors gave their time and special recipes, often with stories and photographs to illustrate what makes them special. And our editor, Olena Seminog, whose idea the book was, has seen it through to completion despite having finished her course, graduated, and started her own family in the United States. That's real dedication! We are grateful to everyone who has had a hand in the book and hope that everyone who reads it will find something of the College in its pages.

Carole Souter
Master
Michaelmas 2017

Preface

The University of Oxford has been teaching students for more than eight hundred years. For much of its history Oxford has been a collegiate university. Thus, every Oxford student belongs to one of the constituent colleges. Oxford teaching and research is widely known, but its dining traditions are less famous. However, with more than forty colleges and private halls catering for the needs of nearly thirty thousand students every day of the term, the culinary tradition at Oxford is not less exciting than the academic.

This book is the first collection of recipes, narratives, photos and drawings by the members of St Cross College. The inspiration for this book came from the delightful meals prepared by the team of chefs working at the College kitchen and the many exciting conversations that I had with students and fellows while eating those meals.

St Cross College was founded in the 1960s to house a growing number of graduate students at Oxford. Since its early years, the College has been known as an egalitarian and inclusive place for British and international students. One aspect that makes St Cross College unlike most other Oxford colleges is that its dining hall and all the dining tables are open to both students and fellows. There is no subdivision, no separate 'high table' only for professors. Here we all eat together and have one joint common room. This encourages conversations and helps to network. For lunches and dinners hundreds of college members head down to a buzzing dining hall. As you enjoy delicious meals and good wine, you meet people and make friends. Therefore, for students, food is an important part of the Oxford experience.

To find recipes for this book, I talked to students, alumni, dons of St Cross College, and their families, and asked them to share the recipes that they relish. None of these people, except for the college chefs, was a professional cook. I consider myself a home-grown gourmet who enjoys dinner table conversations, rather than a trained cook or an experienced book writer. However, after finishing at medical school and completing a doctorate dissertation at Oxford, I do know a thing or two about healthy eating and efficient writing. Although, I have to admit, some recipes in the book are healthier than others.

In this book alongside the recipes, people from sixteen different countries share interesting stories about life and food. A result of this collective effort is a book of recipes as diverse as the people one meets at Oxford. I collected more than fifty recipes many of which have never made it to the cook books. These are the meals prepared at home for people you love. Some recipes are simple, while others require skill and time to prepare.

Among recipes in the book, you can find meals for one, such as a chicken and tomato traybake from the Archeology student Jessye Aggleton, cooked in the basement of student accommodation on Wellington Square in Oxford. At the other end of the spectrum is a meal cooked for Sir David Attenborough, Anthony Geffen, the multiple BAFTA award-winning producer and Fellow of St Cross, and the TV crew working with them, when they were filming a documentary on the Galapagos Islands. The College catering team have provided the recipes for each course of two splendid College feasts: one for Burns' Night, a traditional Scottish celebration, and the other for the dinner celebrating the 50th Anniversary of the College. St Cross College has close physical ties with Pusey House and Pusey Chapel. Their flamboyant junior clergymen provided two cocktail recipes for this book.

By publishing recipes accompanied with personal stories of those who were a part of the University of Oxford, I wanted to offer a fresh look at this prestigious academic institution. Not only is Oxford famous throughout the world, it is also a vibrant and exciting place to study and work. It is a university for bright people of different backgrounds from all over the world. Not every Oxford student will become, or want to become, a prime minister, but they all have the stamina and acumen to succeed at any task they set their mind to, including writing cookery books. My faculty supported me through my doctoral studies, but it was St Cross College that gave me the encouragement and support when I had the idea for this book. Such support for extra-curricular interests is one of the advantages of being part of this collegiate university.

A further reason for writing this book was to learn new recipes, and I definitely succeeded in this. I hope that readers will find many good recipes that they will enjoy cooking at home. To me personally, this book is a memorable souvenir that will always remind me of my Oxford years and the people I met there, wherever life takes me after graduating. I hope that readers too will sense some of the unique Oxford 'vibe' as they read the book, and look through the photos, when choosing a meal to cook.

Olena Seminog, MD, DPhil, FRSA

Acknowledgements

The good food, pleasant surroundings and cheerful company that I found in St Cross College, were an inspiration for this book. It is a pleasure to acknowledge the support and assistance of the College community with collecting the recipes, cooking the meals and preparing the book for publishing. All the stories and recipes in the book were contributed by students, fellows and their spouses, alumni, and the College catering team. The contributors' names are given alongside the recipes. The enthusiasm and support of the College catering team were an inspiration and I would like to acknowledge them specifically: Paul White (General Manager), Robert Rudman (Head Chef), Chris Brook, Daniel Johnson, Dana Lukomska, Iwona Wegeira, Laura Covarrubias, Amanda Clare, and also Darryl Pretorius.

The former Master, Sir Mark Jones, was the first person with whom I discussed the idea of putting together a collection of recipes and stories from the members of the College community. He was positive about the project. I would like to thank him and also the current Master, Carole Souter, and the development officers, Victoria Cox and Ella Bedrock, who gave much of their time in enabling the publication of the book. I thank graphic designer Toby Matthews and The Holywell Press for the design and printing, and John Temple who kindly and freely gave me his advice during the early stages of thinking about the design of the book.

The former Head of the Development Office, Susan Berrington, connected me with Emeritus Fellow Tony Hope. The project gained momentum after my meeting with Professor Hope. If not for Tony, his wife Sally, and their recently extended kitchen, this book would not have happened.

The academic supervisor, mentor and a true Oxford man, Professor Michael Goldacre, gave me freedom to pursue my other interests, including writing this cookery book, as I was working towards completing my doctorate dissertation.

My mother and father, Alla and Alexander Seminog, taught me how to cook, helped to cook some of the meals and take photos that were printed in this book. They also looked after me and my newly arrived baby Aurora as I was finishing the recipe book.

Dr. Olena Seminog

Useful Information

The recipes in this book are from a variety of countries and cultures. Different cultures use different units, and also different ways of specifying quantities. In this book units have been generally left as the authors wrote them.

Abbreviations

g gram(s)
kg kilogram(s)
lb pound(s)
oz ounce(s)
l litre(s)
ml millilitre(s)
°C degrees Celsius (Centigrade)
°F degrees Fahrenheit

Units

1 teaspoon: 5ml
1 dessert spoon: 10ml
1 tablespoon: 15ml
1 cup: 240-250ml
1 oz: 28g
1 lb: 16oz: 450g
1 pint: 570ml
1 litre: 1.76 pints
1 measure of spirits or other alcohol: 25ml

1 cup rice weighs approximately 180g
1 cup flour weighs approximately 120g
1 cup oil weighs approximately 215g

Oven temperatures

100°C	200°F	100°C fan	gas mark ¼
110°C	225°F	110°C fan	gas mark ¼
120°C	250°F	120°C fan	gas mark ½
140°C	275°F	130°C fan	gas mark 1
150°C	300°F	140°C fan	gas mark 2
160°C	325°F	150°C fan	gas mark 3
180°C	350°F	160°C fan	gas mark 4
190°C	375°F	165°C fan	gas mark 5
200°C	400°F	170°C fan	gas mark 6
220°C	425°F	180°C fan	gas mark 7
230°C	450°F	190°C fan	gas mark 8
250°C	475°F	200°C fan	gas mark 9

University degrees

DPhil – Doctor of Philosophy (equivalent to PhD at many universities). A research degree normally taking three years or more full time.

MPhil – Master of Philosophy (generally a two-year Masters involving taught courses and research)

MSc – Master of Science (generally a one-year taught course, or a one-year research degree, in the sciences)

Matriculation – is the formal ceremony that confers membership of the University on students. It normally takes place at the end of the first week of the relevant degree course. The year of matriculation is therefore the year that a student starts a degree course at the University.

St Cross College community – St Cross is a graduate college in the University of Oxford. Its community consists of: current graduate students; current fellows (mainly but not exclusively University academic employees); College staff; alumni (former students); Emeritus fellows (generally retired former fellows) and the St Cross Catering team employed by BaxterStorey.

Pusey House – St Cross College shares a building with Pusey House although the two are quite separate institutions. They share dining facilities and members of Pusey House were invited to submit recipes for this book. The *Sacristan*'s duties involve welcoming new people to Pusey House and organising the services.

Sides, Salads & Starters

Stuffed Vine Leaves

Orly Amali

MSc in Social Anthropology
Matriculation: 1998

Israel

Serves 8-12 people

Cooking time: 75-105 minutes

Pot with a lid

Israel/Palestine

Ingredients

40-60 fresh vine leaves (or preserved, which can be found in Turkish and Moroccan stores)

1 onion cut into cubes

50g pine nuts

1 cup rice rinsed and drained

2 dry apricots cut into cubes

1-2 tablespoons chopped spearmint

1 tablespoon sugar

Juice of 2 lemons (use juice from half a lemon for the filling and the rest for cooking)

1.5 cups of boiling water

1 teaspoon salt

Black pepper

Olive oil

The stuffed vine leaves is my interpretation based on a recipe of an Israeli chef Sherry Ansky, combined with the recipe from "The Gaza Kitchen", and that of Um Ali who is a Palestinian citizen living in Jaffa in Israel and from whom I buy vegetables.

Preparation

1a. When using fresh vine leaves: put them in boiling water for a few seconds, strain and rinse under cool running water.

1b. When using preserved vine leaves: soak the leaves in lukewarm water for 20-30 minutes, drain in a colander and rinse well under cool running water.

2. Heat a pan on low to medium heat and fry the onions in a little olive oil until translucent. Add the pine nuts and fry for a little, add the rice, stir and remove from the heat.

3. Add the apricots, spearmint, salt and pepper to taste, to the pan.
Up to this stage, the filling could be prepared in advance and stored in the fridge for up to 2 days.

4. Add the juice of half a lemon to the filling before rolling the leaves.

Assembling

5. Arrange the vine leaf in front of you, smooth face down. Cut off any remaining stems.

6. Put a tablespoon of the filling along the vine leaf, and roll to the shape of a cigar. Start by covering the bottom, then folding the sides, followed by rolling all the way up. Roll as many leaves as desired.

Cooking

7. Place unused or damaged leaves on the bottom of the pot, to prevent the dish from burning and sticking.

8. Tightly arrange the stuffed leaves in a pot in several layers if required. Spread some olive oil on the top as you arrange the next layer.

9. When all stuffed leaves are arranged in a pot, tighten them up together by placing a plate over the leaves and gently pressing on it.

10. Pour over one and a half cups of boiling water and the juice of one and a half lemons. Add a tablespoon of sugar.
11. Bring to a boil, cover with a lid, and cook on a low heat for 20-30 minutes, until no water is left.
12. Remove from heat and let it stand for another 20-30 minutes.

Serve hot or cold with yoghurt.

Pourgouri Pilaf (Crushed Wheat Pilaf)

Pourgouri pilaf is a couscous-like dish from Cyprus that blends the sweet flavour of chopped fried onion and tomato juice to produce the perfect accompaniment to the pork dish afelia (see recipe: afelia). Greek natural yoghurt is often served with the pilaf, and this introduces moisture to the dry texture of the couscous.

Preparation

1. Finely chop the onion.
2. Heat the oil in a heavy-based casserole (or deep frying pan) and sauté the onions on low to medium heat for 2-3 minutes until light brown.
3. Stir in uncooked vermicelli pasta. Cook with the onions for a couple of minutes until the pasta absorbs the oil and turns a little golden.
4. Squash and break up two chicken stock cubes and place into the casserole. Stir until the chicken stock has dissolved.
5. Add the tomato purée and stir for a couple of minutes on low to moderate heat.
6. Add three cups of water to the casserole. Increase the heat and bring to the boil.
7. Turn down the heat to low to moderate and add the pourgouri. Stir well until homogeneous. Season with salt.
8. Cover and simmer gently for 10-15 minutes or until all the water has been absorbed. Stir well to prevent pourgouri from sticking to the bottom of the pan.
9. Leave the pilaf to rest for 10 minutes before serving.

Sophia Toumazou

DPhil in Zoology
Matriculation. 2013

UK

Serves 3-4 people

Cooking time: 45 minutes

Cyprus

Ingredients

4-5 tablespoons of olive oil

1 large onion

1 cup (100 g) of vermicelli pasta (or you can break spaghetti into smaller pieces)

1½ cups of pourgouri (crushed wheat) – can be found in some supermarkets, if not then try Greek or Turkish food stores

2 organic chicken stock cubes

1 cup of tomato purée or passata (smooth variety)

3 cups of boiling water

Salt to taste

Pan-fried Aubergine with Avocado and Cream Cheese Filling

Olena Seminog

DPhil in Population Health
Matriculation: 2010

Ukraine

Serves 3-5 people

Cooking time: 30 minutes

Ukraine

Ingredients

1 large aubergine

½ avocado

100g cream cheese (such as Philadelphia cheese)

1 tablespoon mayonnaise

1 bunch dill (or any herbs that you like, fresh basil works well)

1 fresh chilli (optional)

Olive oil

Salt

Sugar

Oat biscuits or bread for serving

Many recipes that I know I have learned from my mother. Her family knew about good cooking and good ingredients, and passed this knowledge to her. One of my favourite vegetables to cook and eat is an aubergine, or the eggplant as they call it in North America. Aubergine, which should be called a fruit not a vegetable, has been a family favourite for generations. When my grandfather moved to a small town in Western Ukraine from the sunnier and warmer South East, aubergines were not available and not known in the region. Mother recalls her grandmother making a twelve hour journey on the train to buy and bring the aubergines and the red bell peppers to the family. Although with a certain effort, the family found a way to live their new life in the way they liked it. This story reminds us that simple things like good food and new friends can make life away from home comfortable and enjoyable.

Preparation

1. Wash the aubergine and cut it in rounds of even thickness of about 0.5 cm and season with a little salt on the cutting board. Set aside for 5-10 minutes. Rinse in cold water. Pat dry.
2. In a frying pan heat up two tablespoons of olive oil.
3. Place the aubergine rounds in the pan and fry on each side until cooked (about 2 minutes a side) on medium to high heat. Add more oil if needed.
4. Transfer to a large plate covered with paper towels and let the excess oil get absorbed. Let the aubergine slices cool.

Filling

5. Finely chop the dill.
6. Peel the avocado.
7. Slice the fresh chilli.
8. In a bowl mash the avocado using a fork. Add cream cheese. Mix well. Add dill. Season with salt and a little sugar. Mix well.

Assembling

9. Place aubergine rounds on a large serving plate. Spoon a teaspoon of filling and place it in the middle of each aubergine round. Decorate with the fresh chilli.
10. Serve with the oat biscuits or bread.

 *tip*

Add minced garlic to the filling for a tingly sensation.

Insalata di Rinforzo
(Italian Christmas Salad)

Irene Milana

MPhil in Modern Japanese Studies
Matriculation: 2013

Italy

Serves 4-6 people

Preparation 10 minutes, cooking 1 hour, and 2-3 hours to chill before serving

Italy

Ingredients

1 whole cauliflower
½ jar of your favourite mixed pickles
100g olives
50g capers
50g raisins
Handful of pine nuts
100g anchovies (if you like them)
Extra Virgin Olive oil
Vinegar (your favourite variety)
Salt

My childhood memories of the Christmas holidays start on the morning of the 24th of December with my Grandpa in front of three or four huge pots of boiling cauliflower and a table full of jars of various colourful pickles. By the time we got to dinner those ingredients had been marinating for hours and had turned into his famous 'Insalata di rinforzo' (The Support Salad). We often would have a few different bowls of it because we could never agree on what we would want to have in it, no anchovies for my dad and me, no raisins for my uncle, and so on, and the bowls would be passed around the table until finally the right one reached you.

The great thing about this salad is that Christmas is not a prerogative, but a huge meal is!

We all know the feeling during the festive season when we would really like to have a taste of this and that, but are just too full to have more food. Well, this salad, with the acidity of vinegar and pickles, is just a perfect break between the roast and the stuffing, the pasta and the meat. The recipe is flexible and could be customised to hundreds of variations. Remember that sometimes a good recipe shall be reinterpreted.

Preparation

1. In a large saucepan boil the whole cauliflower until tender. Strain and let cool down.
2. Cut the pickles to bite size and set aside.
3. Cut the cauliflower into big pieces.
4. In a large bowl mix the cauliflower, pickles, olives, capers and raisins together.
5. Sprinkle with a little olive oil, a generous amount of vinegar and add salt to taste.
6. Let rest for a few hours in the fridge and serve at room temperature as a side to the main course.

Beetroot Salad from Australian Coast

The inspiration for this salad was a meal we had in a pub by the coast in Australia. It was the only vegetarian dish available. Beetroot seems to be staging a comeback and this Australian salad was the moment we joined the movement. Fresh beetroot is now (or possibly always has been) widely available in supermarkets when it is in season. This salad is delicious as a light meal on its own, or as a side salad with a robust dish. It keeps well for a couple of days, although it turns pink over time.

Preparation

1. Wrap the beetroots in foil and cook in a conventional oven at 180°C for about 45 minutes to an hour depending on the size of the beetroot, until tender throughout, when a skewer or a fork can be easily pushed to the centre of the beetroot. Unwrap and leave to cool a little. Chop off both ends of the beetroot and peel off the skin.
2. Preheat a pan. Fry the walnuts for a few minutes in the oil until they start to change colour. Take off the heat, cool a little and add the vinegar (it will steam a lot).
3. Once the beetroots are cool enough to handle, slice into wedges. They stain a lot so it is usually best to cut them in the foil, and with rubber gloves.
4. In a bowl mix together the beetroots, baby spinach, and feta cheese. Pour the pan fried mixture of the oil, the vinegar and the walnuts over the salad. Season with salt and pepper to taste (bear in mind that the feta is already quite salty).

Julian Savulescu and Miriam Wood

Julian Savulescu is Fellow of St Cross, Professor of Practical Ethics and Director of the Oxford Uehiro Centre for Practical Ethics

Miriam Wood is Research Development Officer of the Oxford Uehiro Centre.

Australia and United Kingdom

———◆———

Serves 6-8 people

Preparation: 20 minutes; cooking the beetroot 45 minutes

Australia

———◆———

Ingredients

1 bunch of fresh beetroot (usually 4–5 beetroots)

200 g feta cheese

100 g baby spinach

100 g pack of walnuts, roughly chopped

60 ml red wine vinegar

60 ml walnut oil (or olive oil)

Salt and pepper

Potato Salad

Nathan Oesch

DPhil in Experimental Psychology
Matriculation: 2010

United States of America

Serves 6 people

Cooking time: 1 hour

United States of America

Ingredients

8 medium sized white potatoes ('waxy potatoes', preferably not russet potatoes, as they are more for baking)
1 large onion
4 hard boiled eggs
4 celery sticks
400-500 ml mayonnaise
3 tablespoon yellow mustard
Salt
Pepper to taste

My mom used to make this salad every summer in June through August. It was the perfect accompaniment to BBQ: hot dogs, hamburgers, grilled salmon, steak or sausage. Not to forget, a tall glass of fresh-squeezed lemonade. The BBQ was often followed by a swim in Bog Lake, right off the front porch. To finish off, it was typically a slice of fresh blueberry pie and vanilla ice cream which would perfectly seal the deal.

Preparation

1. Peel and boil the potatoes in water for 20-25 minutes until tender but not mushy. Run under cool water, drain in colander and let set until cooled.
2. Chop finely the onion.
3. Cut the eggs and celery into chunks.
4. Cut potatoes into bite-sized pieces.
5. In a large bowl place the eggs, onions, celery and potatoes.
6. In a small bowl prepare the dressing by mixing the mayonnaise and mustard together.
7. Pour the dressing over the potatoes mixture. If it seems a little dry add a little more mayonnaise.
8. Season with salt and pepper to taste. I use quite a bit of pepper.
9. Cover and refrigerate 2-3 hours before serving. Although, can be eaten right away, tastes better if it is cooled for a bit.

Olena's tips

Since my childhood in Ukraine where most salads are mayonnaise-heavy, I have developed a taste for a lighter variation of the sauce in which the mayonnaise is mixed with an equal quantity of sour cream. A sour cream is a healthier alternative for mayonnaise. To make the sauce, whisk together 200 g mayonnaise with 200 g of sour cream, and then mix in the mustard. I also like adding dill and/or capers when I make potato salad and a sprinkling of ground paprika adds a final touch.

Winter Root Vegetable Salad ('Vinaigrette')

Olena Seminog

DPhil in Population Health
Matriculation: 2010

Ukraine

Serves 6-10 people

Cooking time: 90-120 minutes

Ukraine

Ingredients

40-60 fresh vine leaves (or preserved, which can be found in Turkish and Moroccan stores)

1 onion cut into cubes

50g pine nuts

1 cup rice rinsed and drained

2 dry apricots cut into cubes

1-2 tablespoons chopped spearmint

1 tablespoon sugar

Juice of 2 lemons (use juice from half a lemon for the filling and the rest for cooking)

1.5 cups of boiling water

1 teaspoon salt

Black pepper

Olive oil

This is an old Ukrainian recipe. The salad was probably made and served in Eastern Europe long before the refrigerators were invented, at the times when the fruit and vegetables were seasonal and local. Harsh and long winters meant that only limited ingredients, mostly root vegetables and legumes, were available for home cooking. The same ingredients are used for the 'vinaigrette' salad as for the famous Ukrainian meal – beetroot soup (borsch).

In my family vinaigrette was cooked for special occasions. The salad was on the table for the state holidays, both during the USSR and later when Ukraine gained independence, and also during religious celebrations. My family continued rejoicing the important Christian celebrations even during the communist period. However, the traditional recipe has been overshadowed by the more filling Russian salad which contains meat and mayonnaise. This old family recipe came in handy when I decided to become vegetarian. It is full of goodness and comfort that come from the root vegetables seasoned with aromatic sunflower oil and dill. The preparation process involves a lot of cutting the vegetables, but well worth it for the vibrant colour and fabulous taste..

Preparation

1. Wash the vegetables well, but do not peel or cut them.

2. Use two pots to boil the vegetables, one for the potatoes and carrots, and the other for the beetroots. Place vegetables in the pots. Add enough cold water to cover 3-4 cm above the vegetables.

3. Bring pots to the boil on medium to high heat. Then reduce the heat and simmer the vegetables until cooked. The potatoes are likely to be cooked after approximately 15 minutes. Once cooked remove them from the pot with a spoon and continue to cook the carrots which are likely to need a further 5 minutes or so. The beetroots will need about 40 minutes. The vegetables should be soft but not overcooked. To check if a vegetable is ready, push a skewer or a fork through the vegetable: when the vegetables are done they should be soft inside.

4. Discard the water and let the potatoes, carrots and beetroots cool to room temperature.
5. Finely chop half of the onion, and season with salt on the cutting board.
6. Peel the potatoes, carrots and beetroots.
7. Dice the vegetables and the dill pickles in even squares of about 0.3-0.5 cm. The finer they are cut, the tastier is the salad. Transfer to a large serving bowl.
8. Drain the beans. Transfer to a sieve and rinse under cold running water. Drain the water. Add to the bowl.
9. Chop the dill. Add to the bowl.
10. Season with salt and the olive oil or sunflower oil (for more authentic Ukrainian taste).
11. With a spoon lightly stir all ingredients.
12. Serve with the rye bread and smoked salmon.

 *Olena's tips*

I would not recommend to leave cooked vegetables overnight and cut them the next day, because cooked vegetables lose their texture, the potatoes become harder, while the carrots - soggier. My other tip for the best 'vinaigrette' salad is not to peel the vegetables before boiling as they will lose their colour and the potatoes might fall apart while boiling. Finally, a traditional recipe contains pickled cabbage or sauerkraut, however this might not be to everyone's taste.

Pumpkin and Coconut Soup

The taste of a coconut pumpkin soup is a taste of Michaelmas, the start of the academic year, and autumn in Oxford. I made this soup for the first time when I returned home after graduation. The creamy orange texture and warm ginger and coconut flavours reminded me of the lunches in the hall at St Cross. A combination of the flavours, exotic coconut and more traditional pumpkin, reflects the cultural fusion of St Cross College.

Preparation

1. Use a medium sized saucepan. Pour in the water, add the chopped carrots, pumpkin cubes, ginger, rosemary and salt. Bring to boil.
2. Reduce the heat and cook for about 20 minutes partially covered with a lid, or until the vegetables are soft enough to be mashed.
3. Once cooked, remove from heat, drain, discarding the water, and use a fork to mash pumpkin and carrot mix, rather than blending it, to leave some crunchy pieces.
4. Add coconut milk and mix, bringing back to boil.
5. Remove from the heat and sprinkle with some fresh parsley. Taste and season with black pepper, and more salt if required.

Lana Pasic

MPhil Development Studies
Matriculation: 2011

Bosnia and Herzegovina

Serves 4 people

Cooking time: 30 minutes

Fusion

Ingredients

¼ medium-sized pumpkin, cut into cubes
2 medium carrots, cleaned and chopped
2 slices (about 1 cm each) of fresh ginger, peeled
1 litre of water
½ cup of coconut milk
Sprinkle of dried rosemary
Fresh parsley
½ tablespoon of salt
Black pepper

Olena's tips

To release more flavours, sear the vegetables in a generous amount of butter and olive oil on a medium to high heat for about 3-5 minutes, then add water, and cook as described in the recipe.

Chicken Wings Braised in Coca-Cola and Soy Sauce

Sulia Zhong

MSc in Migration Studies
Matriculation: 2014

China

Serves 3-5 people

Cooking time: 35 minutes

Pot with a lid

China

Ingredients

10–20 chicken wings

1 can of Coca-Cola for 10 chicken wings or 0.5 litre bottle for more than 10 chicken wings

Soy sauce

Chicken wings marinated in Coca-Cola is a tasty Chinese dish that is surprisingly easy to make. The American soda beverage became a popular ingredient in Chinese cooking, and is now widely used for cooking sweet-and-sour meat dishes. During my time at Oxford I made this dish for every potluck party we had, and it was everyone's favourite. This ultimate finger food can also be served as a starter or a main dish. The chicken wings can be substituted with chicken drumsticks or pork ribs. Any variety of Coca-Cola would work.

Preparation

1. Rinse well the chicken wings under cold running water (be careful not to spray water from the chicken beyond the sink as chicken skin can harbour pathogenic bacteria). Pat dry. Using a sharp knife make a 5 cm cut on one side of a wing or drumette to enable even cooking and allow the flavouring to penetrate the meat.
2. Put a non-stick pan with high sides on the hob and heat. Put in chicken wings and sear the wings on both sides for two minutes each.
3. In a bowl mix the soy sauce and Coca-Cola in proportion 1:3 to create a sauce.
4. Pour this sauce over the chicken wings so that they are fully covered. Bring to the boil.
5. Put a lid on the pan, reduce the heat to medium-low and simmer for about 15 minutes. Stir occasionally.
6. Take the lid off and increase the heat to medium-high, stirring occasionally, until the sauce is reduced.

Olena's tips

Use Diet Coca-Cola to reduce the sugar load and calories in your meal.

Chinese Dumplings with Pork, Cabbage and Ginger Filling

Sulia Zhong

MSc in Migration Studies
Matriculation: 2014

China

Serves 5-6 people

Cooking time:
Filling must be made at least 6 hours in advance. 1-2 hours (longer if you make the dough from scratch)

Rolling pin

China

Ingredients

Filling
- 225 g minced pork
- 1 onion
- 2 water chestnuts
- ½ medium sized cabbage
- 2 slices fresh ginger
- ½ teaspoon sugar
- 180 ml water
- 1 teaspoon distilled white vinegar
- 1 teaspoon sesame oil
- 15 ml chilli oil
- 15 ml soy sauce
- 75 ml vegetable oil
- 6 g salt

Dough
- 300 g self-raising flour
- 2 eggs
- 2 g salt
- 80-90 ml water

Preparation

Filling

1. Wash the cabbage. Chop finely. Set aside.
2. Mince the ginger.
3. Finely chop the onion and water chestnut. Set aside.
4. Heat oil in a large wok. Turn the heat high and stir-fry the minced pork. Cook until evenly brown. Drain the oil and transfer the pork to a large bowl.
5. Add the cabbage, onions, ginger, water chestnut, salt, sugar and sesame oil to the bowl with minced pork. With a spoon or spatula mix well together. Let rest for 6-8 hours or overnight in the refrigerator.

Dough

You can wrap the filling in premade Wonton skins (Wonton wrappers). However if you prefer to make the dough from scratch, do as follows.

6. Combine the flour, salt and eggs. Mix well.
7. Continue mixing, adding water little by little (about 8 ml) to the mixture until the dough starts to come together. Knead the dough until smooth.
8. Cut the dough into several parts, and then roll each part into 5 cm thick logs. Cut the logs into 5 cm pieces. Using a rolling pin, roll the pieces into round-shaped wrappers.

Assembling the dumplings

The assembling process is the same whether you use homemade dough or Wonton wraps.

9. Open the Wonton wraps and place the wraps on a lightly floured work surface.
10. Scoop a tablespoon of filling and place in the middle of a wrap, leaving the edges free.
11. Wet the tips of your fingers with little cold water and fold the edges of the dough together to form pleats, pinch the edges to lock the filling inside. There is an alternative method for sealing, which is better for boiled dumplings: seal them in a half-moon shape by folding one edge of the dough over another and pinching the edges.

Cooking the dumplings

You can cook the dumplings by pan frying or boiling them.

Pan frying

12a. Heat 3 tablespoons of vegetable oil in a large frying pan on medium heat.

13a. Place the dumplings' bottoms down and fry on each side for 30 – 60 seconds until golden-brown. Keep checking on the dumplings to prevent them from sticking to the pan.

14a. Turn the heat down. Add 180 ml water to the frying pan. Cook covered on low heat for 7-8 minutes until the water starts to simmer. Halfway through cooking add 2 tablespoons of the vegetable oil.

Boiling

12b. Seal the dumplings particularly well in a half-moon shape, as described above, to prevent the dumplings from falling apart while boiling. If they fall apart you will end up with the plain dough circles and filling swimming separately in the boiling water.

13b. In a pot bring water to the boil. When water starts to simmer, put the dumplings in the pot and cook until they float.

14b. Add cold water to keep the water just below boiling while the dumplings are cooking (otherwise they are likely to fall apart).

Sauce for dipping

15. In a small bowl, mix the chilli oil, vinegar and soy sauce together. Make it as hot as personal taste requires.

16. Serve dumplings with the sauce for dipping.

Instead of making the dough yourself you can buy:

- 1 pack (390 g) Wonton skins (Wonton wrappers). You can choose between the squares or circles. The circles are better for boiling.

Smoked Salmon and Cod Mousse Parcels

Jamie Sims

DPhil in Population Health
Matriculation: 2014

UK

Serves 5-7 people depending on the size of ramekins

Cooking time: 75-105 minutes

Ramekins, food processor

Le Mans, France

Ingredients

300g smoked salmon slices (quality is important here)

200g fresh cod fillets

Zest of half a lemon (unwaxed)

1 small bunch of fresh tarragon

250ml crème fraiche

Black pepper

I commenced a DPhil in Population Health in October 2014 to study the long-term health effects of childhood physical activity interventions. I also work as a Senior Lecturer at the University of Chichester, teaching sport psychology and research methods. I am keen on sport and exercise, particularly badminton and outdoor pursuits. Every year, together with my wider family, we go on holiday in the Lake District. During the trip, along with addressing an appetite for peaks, passes and real ales, my family take it in turns to cook the perfect evening meal. This recipe was first attempted following the recommendation of a French guest as it is easy to prepare, elegant, healthy and full of taste.

Preparation

1. Preheat oven to 200°C.
2. Tightly wrap each cod fillet in foil, adding a little butter to prevent sticking.
3. Place fillets in oven and cook for 10 minutes.
4. Remove the cod from the oven and reduce the heat to 150°C.
5. Unwrap the foil and place the warm cod in a food processor. Add crème fraiche, tarragon, lemon zest and pepper to taste. Only add salt if you like it really salty, otherwise there is enough in the smoked salmon slices.
6. Use the slowest setting to mix all the ingredients until only just fully combined, manual pulsing is often easier to control.
7. Thoroughly line the base and sides of the ramekins with the strips of smoked salmon. Do not leave gaps in the lining.
8. Spoon the cod mixture into the lined ramekins and cover with the remaining smoked salmon, cutting to size if required.
9. Place ramekins on a baking tray or directly in the oven and cook for 10 minutes at 150°C to warm through and slightly reduce in size.

10. Remove ramekins from the oven, and gently turn out, or scoop out, the salmon parcels. Serve immediately.

If preparing ahead of time, ramekins filled with cod (step 8) may be covered with Clingfilm and kept for up to two hours. Then, cook and serve as described in steps 9 and 10. The cooking time should be altered accordingly if the ramekins were refrigerated.

Serving suggestions

This is a very versatile and satisfying dish. Choose the size of the ramekins, small or large, depending on whether you are cooking a starter or a main course. Serve on its own or with a salad and chilli salsa, or simply with a lemon wedge. If cooked in a larger ramekin it could be a part of a main course.

There are countless variations of the dish. Try substituting cooked prawns for the cod, including chilli flakes in the mix, substituting a teaspoon of mustard for the lemon zest, or using dill or chives in place of the tarragon.

Olena's tips

This dish is pleasing to the eyes and mouth thanks to a combination of colours and textures, a pink salmon wrapped around white cod mousse. While working on the cookbook, I have cooked this recipe on many occasions, including for a supper at the College chapel for sixteen people. My variation is to add 200 ml of horseradish when blending the cod. This small tweak builds up the flavour of this great meal, and makes the rich fatty salmon taste lighter.

Seared King Scallops

with Charred Onion and Chicken Vinaigrette, Caramelised Onion Puree, Tempura Shallot Rings and Pea Shoots
(The College 50th anniversary dinner starter)

St Cross Catering Team

UK

Serves 6 people

Cooking time: 90-120 minutes

Ingredients

For the scallops
- 6 large diver-caught scallops, with the 'roe' (the pink bit) attached
- Rapeseed oil, for drizzling (or other oil such as olive oil)
- Salt and freshly ground black pepper

For the onion purée
- 50g duck fat
- 600g onions, finely sliced
- 30g unsalted butter

For the tempura shallot rings
- 100g plain flour
- 50g cornflour
- 25g baking powder
- 200ml sparkling water
- Vegetable oil, for deep frying
- 1 shallot, peeled, cut into rings

For the chicken vinaigrette
- 500ml chicken stock
- 50g butter
- Lemon juice
- Salt

Preparation

Scallops

The scallops should be cooked just before serving so prepare all other aspects of your starter first.

1. Trim off any tough, sinewy flesh and remove any black 'veins' from the scallops, but keep the 'roes' (pink sac) intact.
2. Heat a frying pan or griddle pan until hot. Drizzle some rapeseed (or olive) oil over the scallops and season with salt and freshly ground black pepper.
3. Place the scallops on the hot pan or griddle and cook until they are just cooked through, about 2-3 minutes on each side, depending on size. They will feel firm to the touch when cooked. If the scallops are very large, you can finish them in a preheated oven for a few minutes.

On a plate assemble a scallop, onion puré, tempura shallot rings, charred onion, and decorate with pea shoots.

Caramelised onion purée

1. Heat the duck fat in a large saucepan, add the onions and stir well, then cover with a lid. Cook for about five minutes, stirring occasionally, until the onions have collapsed and become translucent.
2. Remove the lid and cook until the onions are a lovely deep golden-brown colour, stirring well to prevent them from catching.
3. Transfer the onions to a blender and blend until smooth. Add the butter and blend again.
4. Remove from the blender to a small saucepan and season. Keep warm until needed.

Tempura shallots

N.B. This recipe uses the technique of deep-frying which involves cooking the shallots in oil at high temperature. This can be dangerous as the hot oil can burst into flames if it comes into contact with the heat source. If you are not experienced in this technique then we recommend that you use a thermostatically controlled domestic deep-frying machine and follow the manufacturer's instructions.

1. Add the flours and baking powder to the sparkling water to form a batter.
2. Heat the vegetable oil to 180°C (350°F).
3. Dip the shallot rings into the batter before deep-frying in the oil for 2-3 minutes, or until golden-brown and crisp. Remove with a slotted spoon and drain on kitchen paper.

Chicken vinaigrette

1. In a saucepan, reduce the chicken stock by two thirds. Once reduced whisk in the butter, add a squeeze of lemon juice and season to taste.

Charred onions

1. Cut the onions in half through the root leaving the skin on.
2. Heat a frying pan and fry the onion halves flesh side down in a little oil, salt and pepper. Fry until the onion is completely black – don't worry, this will give a sweet flavour and will not taste burnt.
3. Turn onto a baking tray skin side down and roast in an oven on 150°C for 15 minutes until soft.

Serving

On a plate, assemble the various parts of this starter. The onion should break down into petals easily. You can use one of the larger petals to hold the chicken vinaigrette.

For the charred onion
- 3 Roscoff onions (or what is available)
- 2 tablespoons of rapeseed oil (or other vegetable oil)
- Salt and freshly ground black pepper

Pea shoots for garnish.

Cock-a-leekie Soup

(Burns' night starter)

- St Cross Catering Team
- Scotland

- Serves 6 people
- Cooking time: 90-120 minutes

Ingredients

- 1 tablespoon vegetable oil
- 1 medium chicken, jointed into pieces (ask butcher to joint chicken if you do not want to do it yourself). If buying chicken pieces in a supermarket buy a mix of leg and breasts and preferably on the bone.
- 180 g smoked bacon lardons
- 2 carrots, chopped
- 2 celery sticks, chopped
- 1-2 leeks, washed and cut into thick rounds (tops reserved)
- Splash of white wine (e.g. 75 mls)
- 2 bay leaves
- ½ bunch thyme sprigs
- 15-20 stoned prunes
- Good-quality bread, to serve

Preparation

NB. Uncooked chicken may contain pathogenic bacteria. Be careful not to transfer bacteria onto kitchen surfaces or food that will not be cooked. If you rinse the chicken be careful not to splash water beyond the sink. If you joint the chicken yourself make sure that all surfaces and knives are carefully washed afterwards. Wash hands after touching the chicken.

1. Heat the oil in a large heavy-based saucepan until hot.
2. Rinse the chicken under cold running water (see note above). Pat dry.
3. Joint chicken into pieces (if butcher has not jointed it).
4. Fry the chicken pieces in batches until golden brown, then remove and set aside.
5. Add the bacon, carrots, celery and leek tops, to the pan in which you fried the chicken pieces, and fry for 5 mins until it all starts to brown. Pour off any excess fat.
6. Splash in the wine and boil rapidly, scraping the bottom of the pan.
7. Return the chicken pieces with the herbs and add enough cold water to cover. Slowly bring to the boil, then simmer for 40 minutes until the chicken is tender.
8. Remove the chicken to a plate, cover with foil and leave to cool slightly.
9. Strain the soup (the liquid from the pan in which you cooked the chicken) into a clean saucepan and discard all the other ingredients.
10. Leave to stand for a few mins and skim off any fat that rises to the top.
11. Pull the meat from the chicken bones and tear into large chunks and put into the soup. Add leeks and prunes.
12. Simmer the soup with the chicken, leeks and prunes for another 20-30 minutes. Season to taste and serve with really good bread.

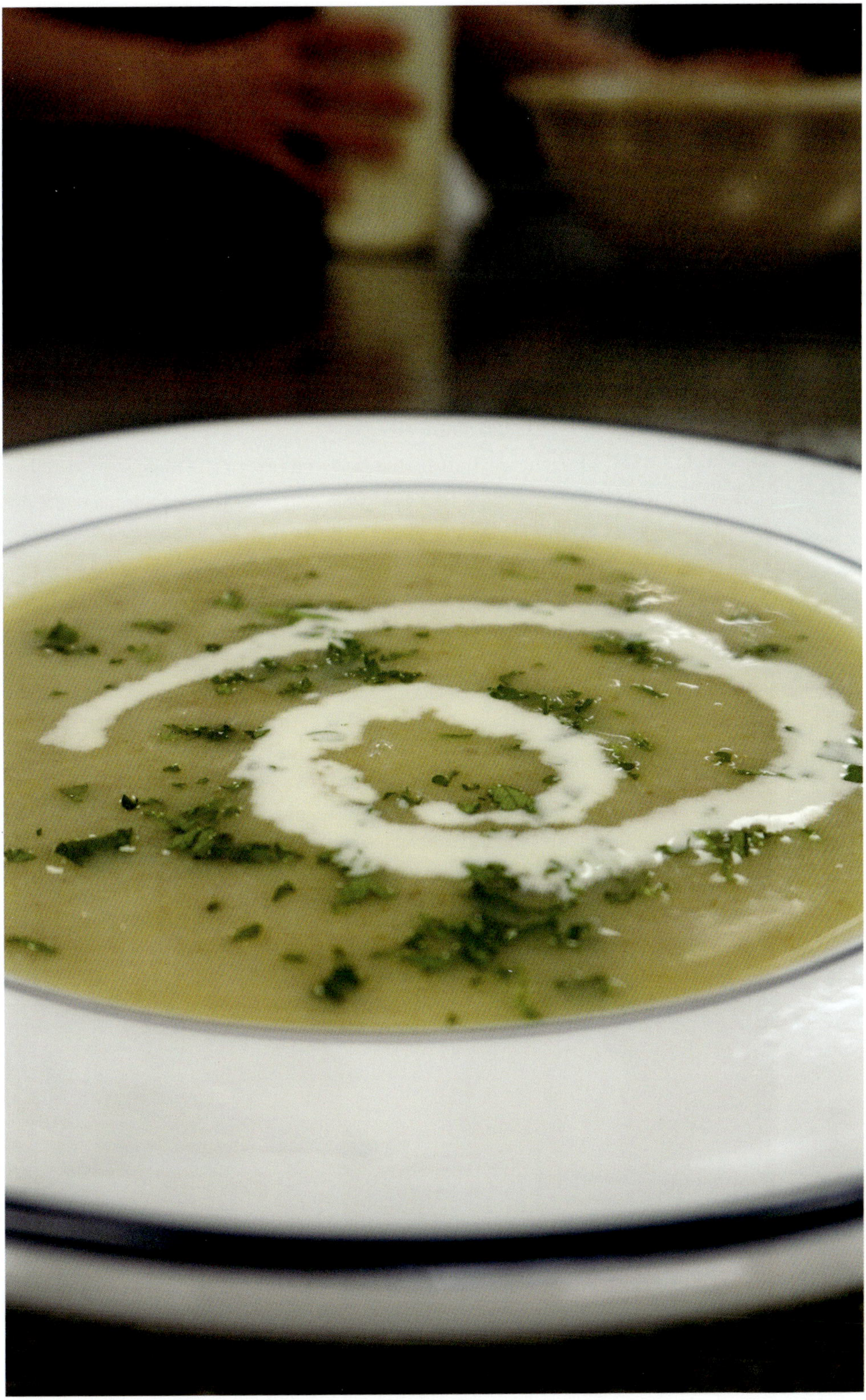

Brown Windsor Soup

Jim Williamson

Senior Fellow
Joined St Cross College in 1970

UK

Serves 4-6 people

Cooking time: 45 mins-1 hour

England

Ingredients

1 kg frying steak
150 g seasoned flour
85 g butter
1 pack thick consommé (e.g. Campbell's concentrated)
250 g mushrooms (sliced)
2 medium onions (sliced)
2 cloves garlic (finely chopped)
250 g sour cream
2 tablespoon grainy mustard

This soup, supposedly created at Windsor Castle, was very popular in Victorian and Edwardian times. It is normally puréed but I prefer to leave it chunky as suggested in Gordon Ramsay's version.

Preparation

1. Heat the oven to 180°C.
2. Cut the steak into strips and toss the strips in the seasoned flour.
3. Heat the butter in a pan and brown the meat.
4. Place meat in a casserole and pour the consommé over.
5. Put the casserole dish in the oven and cook for 1 hour.
6. While the casserole is cooking gently fry the onions and garlic in a pan so that they soften but do not burn. After a few minutes add the mushrooms. Add a little oil if necessary. Cook until soft.
7. When the casserole has been in the oven for an hour, take it out, add the softened vegetables to the casserole, mix well and return the casserole to the oven to cook for a further one hour or until the meat is tender.
8. Remove casserole from the oven. Stir in the sour cream and mustard before serving.

Mains

Porridge with Chia and Coconut Milk

Julian Savulescu and Miriam Wood

Julian Savulescu is Fellow of St Cross, Professor of Practical Ethics and Director of the Oxford Uehiro Centre for Practical Ethics.

Miriam Wood is Research Development Officer of the Oxford Uehiro Centre.

Australia and United Kingdom

Serves 2 people

Cooking time: 15-20 minutes

United Kingdom

Ingredients

40g steel-cut oats

40g oat bran

20-30g raisins (Flame raisins are especially good)

400ml Coconut milk

3 dessert spoons Chia seeds

Porridge in its various forms has seen us through various diet choices: from water-based gruel for low calorie diets to cream and Drambuie calorie-fest on free-for-all weekends. This version has come out of being "vegan-at-home" and is not only the nicest we have tried, but is also the only porridge so far that lives up to the promise of keeping you full until lunch.

Preparation

1. Place the steel cut oats and oat bran, chia and raisins in a heavy-based saucepan and pour over the coconut milk.
2. Cook on a medium heat, stirring all the time. After a few minutes it will start to thicken, and it will continue to do so for several minutes. It is a personal preference as to when you take it off the heat, but we leave it until it keeps its shape in the saucepan, perhaps 6-8 minutes.

Variations

It is also nice served with desiccated coconut on top and non-vegan family members add milk and honey.

Ukrainian Christmas Meal (Kutia)

Kutia is the ultimate Christmas dish in Ukraine just as is Christmas Pudding in England. There are many customs to follow when preparing for, and celebrating, Christmas in Ukraine. First of all, Christmas is celebrated on the 7th of January, not the 25th of December. On Christmas Eve families get together for a festive dinner, and Kutia is one of twelve dishes served. The twelve dishes are a symbolic reminder of the twelve disciples of Jesus Christ. The dinner starts with the first star and Kutia is the first meal served on the night. The custom is to have a meat-free dinner on Christmas Eve, while the meat is reserved for Christmas Day.

My mother makes Kutia with the wheat berries, but I prefer to use the bulgur wheat instead, which makes the cooking process faster and saves me a trip to a Polish store or a large grocery store that sells the whole grain wheat. All other ingredients are easy to find in any food store in England. Kutia tastes great for breakfast on Christmas Day or Boxing Day. If you like the dish, Kutia can become your healthy and filling alternative to porridge for breakfast on any day of the year. Another good thing about Kutia is that it will last for 7-10 days in the fridge, and the flavour only gets better as it sits in the fridge. You can make a large bowl and your breakfast is ready for a week ahead. It is a delightful meal to start the day, the whole grains absorb the sweetness from the

Olena Seminog

DPhil in Population Health
Matriculation: 2010

Ukraine

Serves 8-10 people

Cooking time: 1 hour, preparation 8-12 hours (when using wheat berries)

Food blender

Ukraine

Ingredients

250g wheat berries (or substitute with bulgur wheat)

100g poppy seeds

100g walnuts (keep some for decoration)

50g almonds whole (keep some for decoration)

50g golden raisins

150g honey

50g dried apples

1 fresh apple

30g dried cranberry (optional)

½ teaspoon cinnamon powder

2 tablespoons Sherry (optional)

Salt

honey and the dried berries, and a fresh apple adds a crisp finish. Give this whole food meal a go if you think you need more nutrients in your diet.

Preparation

If using the wheat berries

1. Rinse the wheat in cold water until the water runs clean.
2. Transfer to a bowl and add enough cold water to cover 4 cm above the wheat berries. Soak for 2-3 hours at least or better overnight.
3. Discard the water and transfer the wheat berries to a cooking pot or pan, cover with 850 ml lukewarm water. Bring to the boil on medium to high heat.
4. As soon as the water boils, remove from heat and discard the water. Add 850 ml of lukewarm water again. Add ½ teaspoon salt. Bring to the boil, reduce the heat, and simmer until cooked. The cooking time depends on the quality of the wheat. It may vary between 40 minutes and 1 hour 30 minutes. Check on the water level as you cook, add more if needed. Taste the wheat berries: when cooked they should be soft and tender.
5. Remove from the heat. Discard any excess water. If only a little left, you may keep it. Set aside.

If using the bulgur wheat

1. Place bulgur wheat in a pan. Add 850 ml cold water. Add ½ teaspoon salt. Bring to the boil and simmer for about 10-15 minutes. Remove from the heat.
2. Pour the contents of the pan through a sieve, discarding the water. Rinse the cooked wheat, still in the sieve, under cold running water for 2 minutes. Set aside.

Poppy seeds and honey sauce

1. In a small saucepan place the poppy seeds and add 200 ml boiling water. Cover with a lid and let it sit for 30 minutes.
2. Put the saucepan on a stove, remove the lid. Simmer on low to medium heat until water evaporates. Do not bring to the boil. Remove from the heat, cover with a lid and let it sit for 30 minutes.
3. Rinse well and soak the raisins and dried apples in warm to hot water. Use boiled water, because you will later use some of it for the sauce. Let it sit for 10 minutes or more.
4. Warm up the honey. Place a jar of honey in a bowl or a pot filled with hot water (not so hot as to crack the glass of

the jar). Alternatively, you can microwave the honey, but be cautious as it gets very hot quickly.

5. In a food blender combine the poppy seeds, honey, half of the raisins and half of the dried apples, add the cinnamon powder and Sherry. Run the blender for 2-3 minutes (if the mixture is dry add the water from the raisins).

Nuts and apples

6. Chop half of the nuts.
7. Heat up a frying pan and then put the chopped and most of the whole nuts in the pan (the remaining whole nuts are used for the final decoration – see step 11 below). Toast for a few minutes stirring occasionally until the nuts start to turn golden brown. Remove from the heat.
8. Peel and finely chop a fresh apple.
9. Transfer the raisins and dried apples that were not put in the blender to a sieve and discard the water. Cut the dried apples.

Assembly

10. Transfer all the ingredients (the cooked wheat, all ingredients from the blender, the chopped fresh apple, nuts, raisins and dried apples) to a bowl. With a spoon thoroughly mix together.
11. To serve transfer to a large serving bowl or small individual bowls. Decorate with the nuts.

Olena's tips

The amount of liquid in Kutia depends on personal taste. If you prefer it more watery do not evaporate all the water from the poppy seeds or use the water in which the raisins and dried apples were soaked.

Traditional Ukrainian Varenyky (Pierogi) with Cheese

Liana Semchuk

MPhil in Comparative Government
Matriculation: 2014

United States of America

Serves 4-6 people

Preparation 1 hour, cooking 10 minutes

Ukraine

Ingredients

1 kg potatoes, peeled and quartered

200g medium strength Cheddar cheese, cut into 2.5 cm cubes

4 cups of flour, plus more if needed

1 egg

1 cup water at room temperature

Salt

Varenyky is a Ukrainian staple. Across the country there are many variations of the recipe. Varenyky vary in size, shape and filling. They can be boiled, fried or steamed. Every family has their favourite way of cooking this traditional meal. The filling depends on personal taste, sweet, filled with the cherries, strawberries or other seasonal berries, or savoury, with potatoes, cabbage or cottage cheese.

Preparation

Start by cooking the potatoes, and while the potatoes are boiling, and then chilling, make the dough (steps 6-10).

Filling

1. Peel and cut the potatoes in quarters.
2. Place the potatoes in a saucepan and add cold water to cover the potatoes. Bring to the boil on medium to high heat and then simmer until tender – until a skewer or fork can be pushed easily into the potatoes and the potatoes are starting to fall apart.
3. Discard the water and keep potatoes in the saucepan.
4. Place the cubes of cheese on top of the cooked potatoes and cover with a lid. Let rest for about 5 minutes until the cheese has melted. Sprinkle with 1 teaspoon salt.
5. Mash the potatoes and cheese. Set aside and let it cool to room temperature.

Dough

6. In a large bowl add the flour, egg and half teaspoon of salt and slowly pour in water while mixing the dough until it forms a ball.
7. Place the dough on a floured flat surface. Knead the dough. To prevent sticking, dust your hands with flour before you start kneading and do this again as you go. The dough should have the feel of pizza dough, elastic but not wet. Work in a little extra flour if the dough is too moist.
8. Divide the dough into 3 pieces.

9. Roll out one ball of dough to a thin layer, about 0.3 cm thick.
10. Using a biscuit cutter or a glass, press into the rolled out dough to cut small circles of about 6-8 cm in diameter. Return the leftovers from cutting the circles to the rest of the dough, knead again and reuse.
11. Place a dough circle in your hand and spoon about a heaped tablespoon of filling into the middle of the dough, leaving the edges empty.
12. Pull the dough over the filling and pinch the edges. If the dough is dry, moist your fingers in cold water to help seal the edges. In Ukraine the filled pastry is called *varenyky* [vɑˈɭɛniːkiː].
13. Sprinkle a tray with flour and place the varenyky on it.
14. Repeat process (steps 11-13) for all the dough circles.
15. In a large saucepan boil the water with a pinch of salt and place varenyky in boiling water for about 8-10 minutes. They rise to the surface when cooked.

Serving suggestions

Varenyky tastes really good served hot with bacon and/or sour cream. Cut the bacon into 1-2 cm strips and fry until browned and crisp. Toss cooked varenyky in bacon and bacon grease. You could top it with sour cream.

Smachnogo! (Bon Appetit in Ukrainian)

Olena's tips

To store varenyky, freeze the uncooked varenyky, and later cook from frozen. Ideally, for freezing you would place varenyky on a flat surface, for example a cutting board, sprinkled with flour, leaving enough space in between each, so that they do not stick to each other. After varenyky are frozen hard, you can place them in a more convenient storage container, and put back in a freezer. Be quick and do not defreeze varenyky as you transfer them, otherwise you have to cook them right away.

Taboulé

Orly Amali

MSc in Social Anthropology
Matriculation: 1998

Israel

Serves 2-4 people

Preparation time:
20 minutes. Cooking time:
10 minutes. 8-12 hours to soak the bulgur wheat

Palestine/Lebanon

Ingredients

200-350g coarse bulgur wheat

½-1 bundle of mint

½-1 bundle of flat parsley (not the curly one)

½-1 bundle of spring onions (thin green leaves)

1 ripe tomato

50-100g pine nuts

2-3 lemons (juice only)

Olive oil
(a variety with a strong taste and aroma, Middle Eastern style, found in Lebanese & Moroccan stores would work the best here).

Atlantic sea salt, also called Celtic

This Taboulé is one of my early culinary highlights. Some of my close friends in Oxford had the opportunity to taste it about eighteen years ago. It is my personal take on the Palestinian-Lebanese recipe that is made with bulgur wheat, rather than semolina as in the Maghreb.

Preparation

1. Soak bulgur wheat in cool water for about 6 hours, changing water several times until clean.
2. Rinse the wheat under cool running water, strain in a colander, if required, squeeze with your hands to get excess liquid out. Place in a dry bowl.
3. Cover with cling film and put in the fridge for several hours. Ideally, let it stay overnight.
4. Wash mint, parsley and spring onions. Let dry and then divide leaves from stems.
5. Roast the pine nuts until golden in the oven at 150-180°C. Be very careful and attentive as they tend to turn from golden to 'burnt' in seconds.
6. Finely chop the greens with a sharp knife in the following order: spring onions, parsley, mint (mint last as it quickly turns black) and add to the bowl with bulgur.
7. Wash and finely chop the tomato and add to the bowl.
8. Season with plenty of olive oil, salt and lemon juice. Start with half quantities and add more as desired.
9. Add the roasted pine nuts and serve at room temp.

If stored in the fridge, take it out one hour before eating, taste and adjust seasoning as desired.

Variations

You can add to the basic recipe pomegranate seeds, barberries, fresh coriander, pickled lemons, Sumac or finely chopped sundried tomatoes.

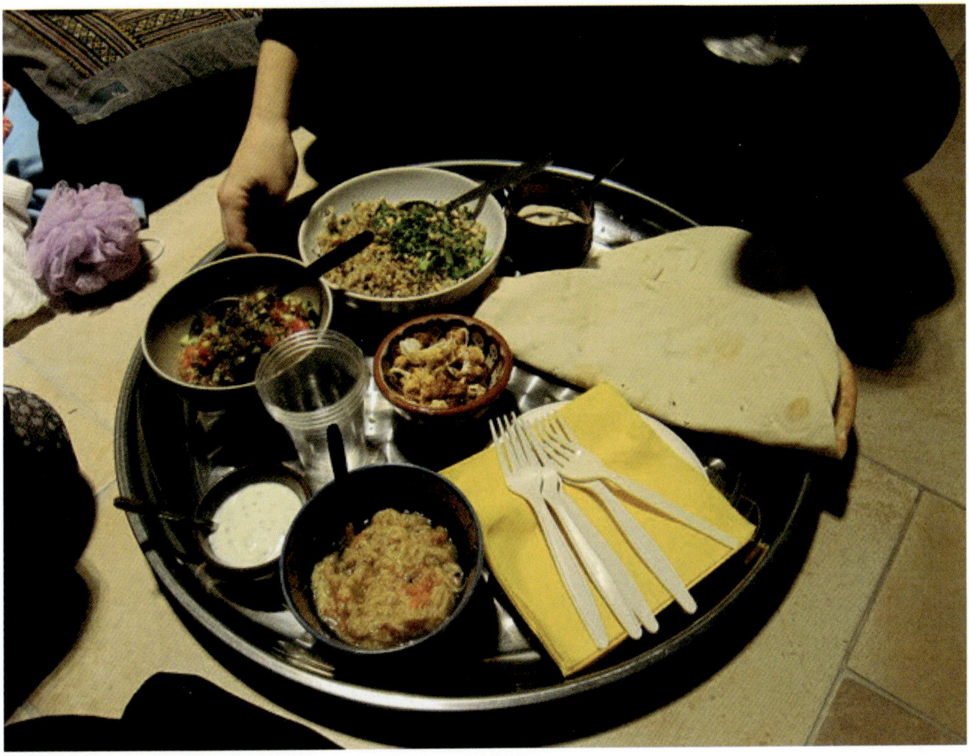

Bibimbap

(Korean Mixed Rice with Assorted Vegetables)

Peter Fiske

DPhil in Archaeology
Matriculation: 2011
Student President: 2012-2013
Student Dean: 2013-2015

Greece and the US

Serves 3 people (or 2 students!)

Cooking time: 40 minutes – 1 hour

10 small to medium-sized bowls

Korea

Ingredients

200g Thai fragrant rice
Miso soup (optional)
Kimchi (optional)
1 egg per guest
Frying oil

Gochujang sauce
- 3–4 generous tablespoons gochujang (red chili paste)
- 1–2 tablespoons minced garlic
- 2 tablespoons sesame oil
- 2 tablespoons roasted sesame seeds
- 1 tablespoon rice wine vinegar
- 1 tablespoon sugar (optional)

Vegetable mix
- 200g shiitake mushrooms
- 200g carrots (1 medium size)
- 300g courgette/zucchini (1 medium size) or cucumber, depending on preference
- 300g bean sprouts
- 300g spinach
- 300g tofu (recommended, but optional)

Seasoning for spinach and bean sprouts
- 3 chopped spring onions
- 1–2 teaspoons minced garlic
- 3 tablespoons sesame seeds (or more)
- 3 tablespoons sesame oil

Bibimbap has been one of my perennial favourites since my time as an undergraduate at Berkeley. Oxford had been bereft of Korean restaurants until 2013, when Bamboo opened near the train station. A year later, my sister-in-law and brother arrived in Oxford for a research fellowship, and we had one of our first meals together there. Reminded of her own love for the dish, and of how healthy it can be, she began experimenting with variations based on numerous sources from books and found online. Along with a great deal of Middle Eastern cooking, this dish has become a staple of our weekends together, chances to come together as a family and fortify ourselves for the week ahead. The following recipe is hers. There are several variations of the recipe, including with bulgogi, but the vegetarian version is delicious and is included here. It has been modified slightly to adjust for the difficulty in finding some of the traditional Korean vegetables here in Europe, but you are encouraged to find them and try them if you can.

The ingredients in the bibimbap and their colours have symbolic meaning. Shiitake mushrooms, coded as black, stand for the North (kidneys). The carrots, coded as orange/red, stand for the South (heart). The spinach and the courgettes stand for the East (liver). The bean sprouts and the tofu stand for the West (lungs). The egg stands for the Centre (stomach). Overall goodness.

Preparation

Make sure you have about 10 small to medium-sized bowls to store different ingredients as you cook.

1. In a bowl mix together gochujang, minced garlic, sesame oil, sesame seeds, vinegar and sugar. Set aside. This mix is the Gochujang sauce.
2. Wash all the vegetables and mushrooms. Peel the carrot and the courgette. Cut the carrot in short thin strips. Set aside. Slice the courgette. Set aside. Slice the shiitake mushrooms and slice thinly. Set aside.
3. Slice the tofu.
4. Prepare the seasoning for spinach and bean sprouts. In a bowl mix together half of the chopped spring onions, minced garlic, sesame seeds and sesame oil. In another bowl mix the other half of the ingredients. Set aside the two bowls.
5. In a pot heat enough water to cover the spinach (but do not yet add the spinach). When the water is boiling, toss in the spinach and cook for 2–3 minutes. Drain and run under cold water for about 2 minutes. Squeeze out the water.
6. Add the spinach to one of the bowls with seasoning and toss (mix) well. Set aside.

7. In a pot heat enough water to cover the bean sprouts (but do not yet add the sprouts). When the water is boiling, toss in the bean sprouts and cook for 3-4 minutes. Drain and run under cold water for about 3-5 minutes.

8. Add the bean sprouts to the second bowl with seasoning (not the one with the spinach) and toss (mix) well. Set aside.

9. Cook the rice in the rice cooker or boil in a pot. Follow the cooking instructions provided on the rice packaging.

10. In a wok or a pan heat up a tablespoon of cooking oil. Fry carrot strips on medium to high heat for about 2-3 minutes until they are mildly softened. Season with salt as you cook. Take carrots off the heat, drain off the oil and transfer the carrots to a bowl. Set aside. Do not turn the heat off.

11. Add more oil and fry the courgette slices. Cook each side for about 2-3 minutes until the slices are slightly charred and starting to curl up. Take off the heat, drain the oil and transfer the courgette slices to a bowl. Set aside.

12. Add a tablespoon of oil to the wok or pan and fry the tofu slices. Cook on each side for about 5 minutes until golden. Set aside.

13. Add a tablespoon of oil to the wok or pan and fry the shiitake mushrooms for about 2-3 minutes until cooked. Take off the heat, drain the oil and transfer the mushrooms to a bowl. Set aside.

14. If using miso soup, bring water to the boil (for quantities follow instructions on the packaging). Empty one sachet of soup per person in a small bowl, add the water, mix well.

Assembling and serving bibimbap

Serve bibimbap in a large bowl, with enough room to mix the ingredients and sauce together. Divide all ingredients that you set aside in small bowls in equal amounts between two or three serving bowls depending on the number of guests.

Assemble each individual bowl as follows. On a bed of rice arrange in circular fashion the spinach, the bean sprouts, the carrots, the shiitake mushrooms, the courgettes, and the tofu.

Just before serving fry one egg per guest (sunny side up). Preserve the shape of the egg. Put the egg on top of the assorted vegetables and tofu.

Present the bowl with all the ingredients arranged in a circle with an egg on top. Add as much Gochujang sauce in each bowl as desired. You can add the sauce gradually to adjust the spiciness to personal preferences. Mix everything together before eating.

Serve, if desired, with kimchi and miso soup on the side. Miso soup can be poured over bibimbap and mixed in.

Lasagne

Preparation

Cheese Mixture

1. In a large bowl beat the eggs. Fold in all ricotta cheese and parmesan, and half of the mozzarella cheese to form the 'cheese mixture'. If using dried basil add this to the mixture and stir in gently.

To Assemble

2. Heat oven to 190°C while assembling the dish.
3. Grease a 33 × 22 cm ovenproof dish with butter.
4. Cover the bottom with a layer of lasagne sheets (3-4 pieces) lengthwise.
5. Spread about 1/3 of the tomato sauce over the lasagne sheet.
6. Spoon and layer about 1/3 of the cheese mixture on the top of tomato sauce. If using fresh basil leaves then distribute 1/3 of them roughly evenly over the cheese mixture.
7. Repeat steps 4-6 to form a second layer.
8. For the last third layer place the lasagne sheets over the second layer, then spread the remaining 1/3 of the cheese mixture over lasagne sheets, and then the last 1/3 of the tomato sauce (and remaining fresh basil leaves if using these).
9. Spread the remaining 450 g of mozzarella cheese evenly on top.
10. Cover the ovenproof dish with aluminium foil and bake for 50-60 minutes. The casserole should be bubbling.
11. Remove foil for the last 5 minutes of cooking so cheese gets slightly brown.
12. Remove casserole from oven and let stand 15 minutes before trying to cut into slices.

Nathan Oesch

DPhil in Experimental Psychology
Matriculation: 2010

United States of America

Serves 6-8 people

Cooking time:
1 hour 30 minutes

Italy

Ingredients

1 box lasagne sheets

500 ml tomato sauce (or 2 jars of Ragu or Prego spaghetti sauce)

450 g ricotta cheese

900 g shredded mozzarella cheese

250 g grated parmesan

3 eggs

20 g butter

10-20 fresh basil leaves (if you can find them) otherwise 2 tablespoons dried basil

Tip

For a meaty lasagne add cut sausages or hamburger meat to the tomato sauce.

Spicy Vegetarian Chili

Nathan Oesch

DPhil in Experimental Psychology
Matriculation: 2010

United States of America

8-10 people

Cooking time: 1 hour

5.5-7 litre Dutch oven or a large saucepan with lid

United States of America

Ingredients

500g fresh aubergine (eggplant), cut into 2.5 cm cubes

2 white onions, chopped

3 cloves garlic, minced

2 medium courgettes (zucchini), chopped

2 large red bell peppers, cored, seeded, diced

1 to 2 jalapeño peppers (chillies), seeded, finely minced (taste and check the heat of the jalapeños. If very hot only use one; if mildly hot, use two. Wash hands with soap and water after handling. Do not rub eyes.)

800 g (2 cans) Italian plum tomatoes, coarsely chopped, including liquid (or 1 kg of fresh plum tomatoes, peeled and chopped)

½ cup cooked white beans

½ cup cooked kidney beans

Zest of one lemon

3 tablespoons lemon juice

1 tablespoon ground cumin

1-2 tablespoons chilli (chili) powder

2 tablespoons chopped fresh oregano or 2 teaspoons of dried oregano

1 teaspoon fennel seeds

⅓ cup chopped fresh cilantro (coriander) or you can substitute with parsley

1 teaspoon sugar

Olive oil

Salt and freshly ground black pepper to taste

My mom used to make these over chilly winter nights in January and February. Growing up as a kid in Maine, I was often a rather reckless and irresponsible child. Occasionally, I would go without footwear, running around barefoot in the snow, making snowmen and snow angels. But before too long, I would inevitably need to come inside for a cup of hot chocolate, with feet under a warm blanket. Come dinner time, a hot cup of chili, or a warm slab of lasagne, would definitely hit the spot and warm the soul.

Preparation

1. Preheat oven to 180°C.
2. Scatter aubergine cubes in a shallow roasting pan and slather with 2 tablespoons of olive oil. Cover the pan with aluminium foil and bake for about 30 minutes, stirring once during the cooking. Remove from the oven and set aside.
3. In a large thick-bottomed Dutch oven (or saucepan), heat 3 tablespoons of olive oil on medium heat. Add the onions and cook for about 4 minutes, or until translucent. Add

the garlic and cook for one minute until fragrant. Add the red bell peppers, courgettes, and jalapeño chilli peppers. Cook for about 5 more minutes, stirring occasionally.

4. Add the chopped tomatoes to the pot along with any liquid that may have been in the can. Add oregano, cumin, and fennel seeds. Add chilli powder to desired heat.
5. Stir in the aubergine cubes (carefully so as not to break them up), and simmer for 20 minutes over low heat.
6. Add the white beans and kidney beans, lemon zest, lemon juice, sugar, and chopped cilantro (coriander). Add salt and freshly ground pepper to taste. Simmer for 5 minutes.

Serving suggestion

Serve with sour cream, grated cheddar cheese, and chopped green onions.

Tip

The level of spiciness will depend on how much chilli powder, and how many jalapeños you put in the chilli. If you like things on the mild side, start with the smaller amounts of both, and add to taste.

Upgraded Ready-Made Curry

Martin Vessey

Emeritus Fellow of St Cross College, Emeritus Professor of Social and Community Medicine

A Fellow of St Cross College from 1973

UK

Serves 2 people

Cooking time: 10 minutes

Oxfordshire, England

Ingredients

Sainsbury's curries which come in a pack with rice on one side and the curry on the other. (Choose the ready-made curry of your choice from your local supermarket or other shop)

2 teaspoons olive oil

Mushrooms (quantities as desired – perhaps six button mushrooms)

Tomatoes (quantities as desired – perhaps four medium sized)

(Optional) Extra frozen meat or seafood; or leftover meat or seafood.

My wife Anne and I first learned about the joys of curry when we lived in Harpenden some 50 years ago. We were taught an excellent, if complicated, recipe by a young Indian Church of England curate whom we got to know well. However, the incentive to make the curry was gradually lost as our family grew; in general, young children don't like curry and there isn't much time for fancy meals anyway! In addition, caution is needed if curry is to be served to dinner guests because some people definitely don't like it. Usually it is much safer to go for a rather more bland dish. Sadly, we lost the curate's recipe as a consequence of non-use.

I have to admit that, in fact, I made very little input into cooking while we still had children at home and while I was still working (very) full time. Years later on a shopping expedition with Anne when I was less pressed for time and there were only the two of us to feed, I discovered Sainsbury's delicious pre-made frozen curries.

As for my curry recipe the facts are simple (a) I love curry and Sainsbury's do a good job (b) I am lazy, especially when it comes to cooking (c) Anne and I always have supper together when we are both at home (d) Sainsbury's curries of "the rice included" type will not feed two (certainly not if I am around) (e) Therefore a simple solution is required (f) I have risen to the occasion with a minimum amount of personal effort – satisfaction all round!

This is probably a totally useless recipe but I wanted to offer something for the College cookbook. Furthermore, there will probably be other fairly hopeless cooks who look at this book and who like curry.

Preparation

1. Cook a curry from frozen in a microwave. Give the pack an initial 4-5 minutes at full strength to melt both rice and curry (or follow manufacturer's instructions).
2. Remove the rice and put it in a separate dish.

3. Add 2 tablespoons of water to the rice; mix the water in; and cover the dish with cling film.
4. Give the rice another 1-2 minutes of microwaving.
5. Divide the contents of the 'curry side' (i.e. the ingredients other than the rice) of the original container into two parts. One part is left where it is and the other half is placed in the other side of the container previously occupied by the rice.
6. Add about one teaspoonful of olive oil to each side of the container and mix the curry up.
7. If the curry is a fish (or prawn) one, add some additional (frozen) seafood (we always keep a pack in the freezer). If the curry is a chicken one, add some cooked chicken bits or frozen chicken if you have any to hand.
8. Add chopped up fresh tomatoes and chopped up fresh mushrooms to each side of the curry pack and mix together the contents of each side of the pack.
9. Cover the curry pack with cling film and microwave for 2-3 minutes (or longer consistent with the instructions on any additional frozen food added).
10. Microwave the dish holding the rice for about another minute.
11. All is then ready to serve onto pre-warmed dishes. It tastes great, there is enough of it for two, it has been easy to prepare and both my wife, Anne, and I are happy!

Curry with Lamb and Prunes

Sunil K. Sukumaran

DPhil in Organic Chemistry, Dyson Perrins Laboratory
Matriculation: 1990

India

Serves 6-8 people

Cooking time: 45 min – 1 hour preparation

Heavy-bottomed pan with a lid

India

Ingredients

1 kg lamb, cut into 7 cm pieces with bones

3 tablespoons oil

40g butter (or ½ cup of Ghee or clarified butter)

8 green cardamoms

4 cloves

4 x 5 cm cinnamon sticks

6 peppercorns

6 garlic cloves

3 teaspoons Cayenne pepper powder

2 teaspoons turmeric powder

30g tamarind paste (if tamarind paste is not available, dissolve 3 tablespoons of brown sugar in 4 tablespoons of vinegar, or use juice of one lemon instead of vinegar)

1 cup prunes (substitute with dried apricots)

Salt to taste

I was introduced to this recipe by an old family friend, Rocky Mohan, whose family makes India's famous rum "Old Monk". For many years it was the largest selling brand of dark rum in the world. Ironically, Rocky is mostly a teetotaller but remains a passionate foodie, gourmet, and a curator of fine recipes. He has authored many books on Indian food, and his knowledge of Indian spices and cooking techniques is vast.

This recipe is from Kashmir, and the dish is part of the Wazwan, an elaborate multicourse meal. The Royal Wazwan's scale has vastly diminished from the mighty seventy-two course meal it used to be to a mere forty course meal nowadays. Guests are seated in the groups of four and share the meal from a large silver plate, Tarami, covered with fragrant white rice.

Before the feast starts, an attendant carrying an ornate splayed-out copper vessel, Tasht-Nari, walks around and offers each guest a ceremonial washing of the hands, as the meal is traditionally eaten by hand. Then, the feast begins.

Preparation

1. Disperse Cayenne pepper powder in ¼ cup of water.
2, Make a paste of garlic cloves.
3. Warm the oil and butter in a heavy-bottomed pan over medium heat. Add the cardamoms, cloves, cinnamon sticks, peppercorns, and stir for a minute. Add the garlic paste, and stir for a minute. Add the lamb pieces and cook for a few minutes, stirring if necessary, to brown the lamb pieces on the outside.
4. Pour water with Cayenne pepper over meat.
5. Season with salt to taste (about 1.5-2 teaspoons).
6. Cook on high heat for 10-15 minutes or till oil separates. Add water to cover the meat, put the lid on the pan and cook until the meat is tender. Add more water if required.

7. Add the tamarind paste, turmeric powder, and dried prunes. Stir well and simmer for 8-10 minutes till the plums have softened.
8. Taste and adjust the salt.
9. Serve hot with steaming rice or hot roti (chapati, flat bread).

Olena's tips

For a smaller party, use half the ingredients and adjust the spices and cooking time accordingly. This recipe can be easily adapted for vegetarians by substituting the lamb with Quorn minced meat. It only takes 7-10 minutes to make a vegetarian alternative of the curry.

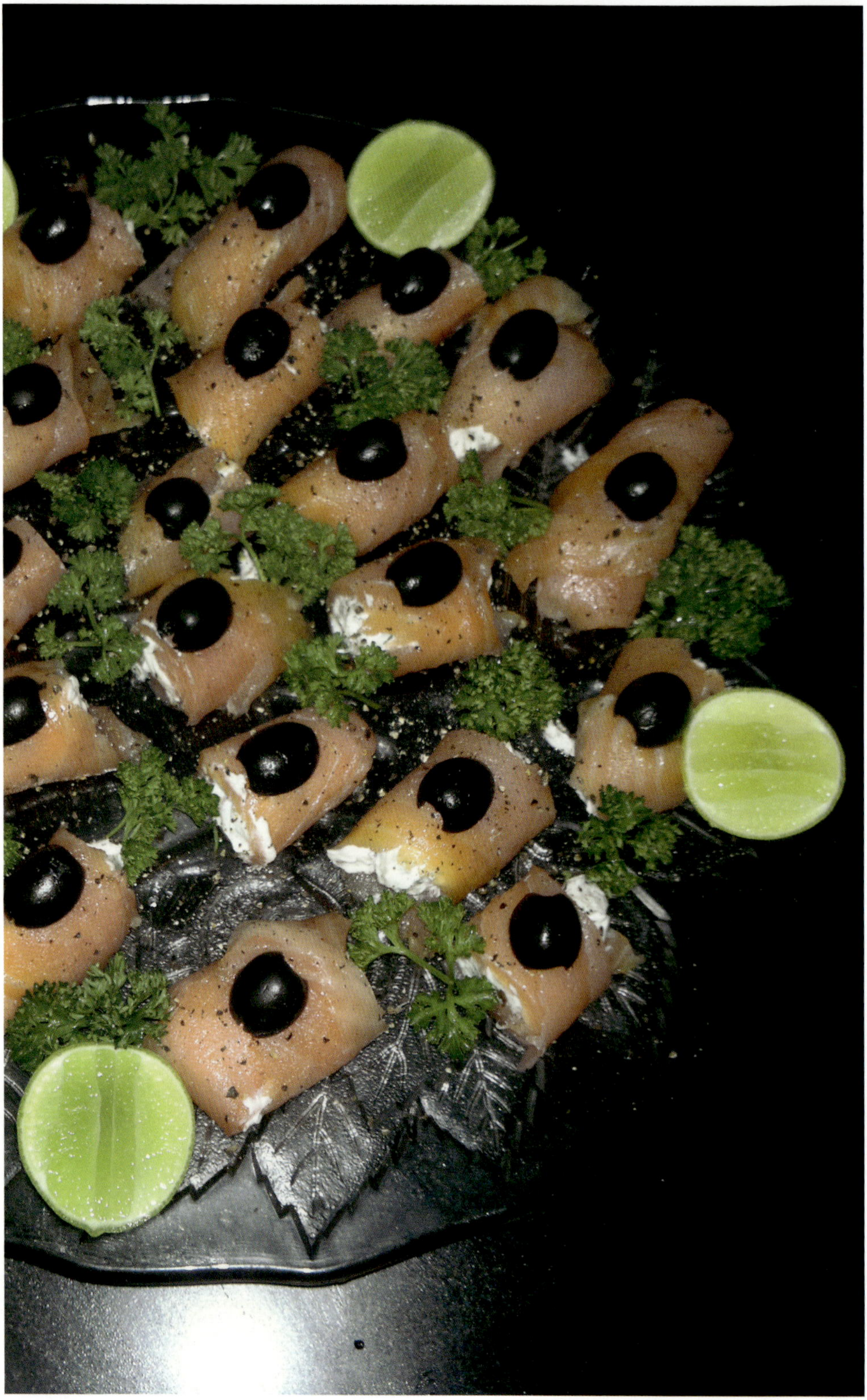

Salmon Rolls with Cream Cheese

Preparation

1. In a bowl, mix the cream cheese, crème fraîche and olive oil.
2. Finely chop the olives, capers, shallots and dill. Add to the cream cheese mixture. Season with black pepper and gently mix until all the ingredients are combined.
3. Lay the smoked salmon on a flat surface. Evenly spread the cheese filling on top of salmon using a spatula.
4. Roll each slice of salmon in the same way as a Swiss Roll is rolled.
5. Cut each roll into inch-length (2.5 cm) pieces.
6. Arrange rolls on a platter, squeeze a lemon or half a lime on the rolls, and season with freshly ground pepper. Garnish with the parsley, black olives and lime wedges.

Serving suggestions

Serve with Melba toast, which can be made by toasting very thin slices of white bread, or by toasting slices of white bread and then cutting each slice in half to create a very thin slice, and toasting (grilling) the untoasted side.

Sunil K. Sukumaran

DPhil in Organic Chemistry, Dyson Perrins Laboratory
Matriculation: 1990

India

Serves 6-8 people

Cooking time: 20-30 minutes

India

Ingredients

350 g of sliced smoked salmon

250 g cream cheese

100 g crème fraîche

12 black olives pitted

2 tablespoons capers

6 small shallots (or 1 medium onion)

2 tablespoons extra-virgin olive oil

1 bunch of dill

1 lemon or lime

Freshly ground black pepper

Parsley, black olives, wedges of lime for garnishing

Nellie Shackelford Saunders' Chesapeake Bay Crab Cakes

Jordan McKittrick

MSc in Physical and Theoretical Chemistry
Matriculation: 2014

United States of America

Serves 4-8 people

Preparation: 15 minutes; cooking: 5-10 minutes; and 1-8 hours to rest in the fridge before cooking

United States of America

Ingredients

- 125 ml Panko bread crumbs or equivalent amount of crushed low-fat cream crackers (crushed Saltines in the US)
- 75 g mayonnaise
- 50 g Dijon mustard
- 1 large or 2 medium sized eggs
- 2 or 3 green (spring) onions,
- 500 g jumbo lump blue crab meat
- Oil (preferably peanut oil) for frying or 125 ml (100 g) butter for grilling

Nellie Shackleford Saunders was my maternal grandmother's mother and was born and raised in Tidewater, Virginia, where the James River, the Chesapeake Bay, and the Atlantic Ocean come together. Her family had been eating Chesapeake Bay crabs for generations, potentially as early as the late 1630s, when her family originally settled in Tidewater. Not long before King Charles I escaped to Oxford, some in the King's Court who had been gifted land in Virginia decided to flee across the Atlantic. I would like to think that my umpteenth great grandfather, who was one such Royalist, was so desperate when he arrived in the wilderness of Gloucester, Virginia, that he ventured to eat these sea spiders we now call Blue crabs.

When I was a young boy, I would catch crabs by stuffing bait fish into a crab pot and tossing the pot into the river that runs behind our house and empties into the Bay. After steaming the crabs, we could pick the meat out directly, which involved covering the porch table with newspaper, spreading the crabs on top, and cracking them open by hand. For lunch it was common to eat crab like this, but for supper, my mother would make sides such as spoon bread (similar to a rich corn soufflé) and collard greens with ham and would use the meat to make crab cakes. Regardless of when the traditions began, crabs have been a family staple for a long time. They are far more than mere food: like the generations before me, they represent endless memories on the water surrounded by family and friends.

Preparation

1. Chop the green onions finely, white and green parts included.
2. In a large bowl, mix together well the crumbs or crushed crackers, mayonnaise, mustard, eggs, and onions.

3. Gently fold in the crabmeat, avoiding breaking the lumps apart. With your hands, gently pat together 8 rounded patties. Avoid flattening them too much.
4. Cover a cutting board or a tray with a grease-proof paper. Place the crab cakes, cover and refrigerate for an hour or up to 8 hours. Refrigerating will help to hold the patties together and keep the texture of the crab meat intact.
5. Crab cakes could be pan fried or grilled.

Frying
6a. Add enough peanut oil to make a depth of about 1.5 cm in a frying pan. Turn the heat high. Fry quickly in a very hot oil, turning once, until brown, for about 5 minutes total.

Grilling
6b. Place cakes on an aluminium foil-lined baking sheet. Melt about 125 ml of butter and baste the cakes with the butter. Grill on the top shelf of the oven for about 4 to 5 minutes, watching carefully so they don't burn.

Serve cold or hot. Optional serve with caper sauce. For the caper sauce mix equal amounts of mayonnaise and soured cream, add drained capers, chopped fresh parsley and chive, olive oil and lemon juice.

Olena's tips

Although the original recipe indicates using the blue crab meat, depending on where you are in the world, try to substitute it with a locally sourced crab meat. In Oxford we tested this recipe with two different types of crab meat, a blue crab and a local Cornish crab. Both varieties of the crab meat worked nicely in this recipe. Between three of us in the tasting party we could not agree on which one worked better. Bear in mind, if you are in the UK, the crab meat from the English coast, although not cheap, would cost you half the price of the blue crab. The taste of the mayonnaise is important in this recipe so buy good quality or make your own.

Basque Cod with Pil Pil Sauce

- Veronica Walker Vadillo and Goiz Ruiz De Gopegui
- DPhil in Archaeology Matriculation: 2011
- Spain and United States of America

- Serves 4 people
- Cooking time: 45 minutes-1 hour for cooking. If you use salted cod allow 48 hours to de-salt
- Large pan (preferably ceramic, but metallic is also fine)
  Metallic kitchen sieve
- Bilbao, Basque Country

Ingredients

- 8 pieces of cod loin (salted cod is ideal, but fresh cod could be used instead)
- 1 cup extra virgin olive oil
- 5 garlic cloves sliced
- 3 dry Cayenne peppers

Olena's tips

Do not let the apparent complexity of the Pil Pil sauce stop you from cooking this Basque dish. The slow cooked cod is delicious on its own even without the sauce. As you practice, you will master the art of cooking the Pil Pil sauce.

Getting accepted to do a DPhil at the Oxford Centre for Maritime Archaeology was a life changing event not only for me, but also for my husband. We anticipated a risk of having to live apart for the duration of the doctorate. Luckily St. Cross College provides graduate family accommodation, so we moved to Oxford together. During the first year I focused on my research, and my husband took a gap year to relax and practice one of his best skills – cooking.

There are not that many things in the world that can lift up your spirits better, when you are a student and particularly when you have the dreaded writer's block, than the smell of freshly cooked food. My husband has started a full-time job after a year, but carried on with cooking for the family. Of all versatile meals he has cooked since we moved to Oxford, cod fish in Pil Pil sauce is probably the most favourite.

The cod in Pil Pil sauce is a traditional dish from the Basque country. As the local legend says it goes back to the 19th century, when the population of the city of Bilbao were under siege during the Carlist wars. There was a shortage of food, but plenty of time to spare for cooking and truly enjoying the little pleasures that were available. From this dramatic historical event came an ingenious recipe to make a delicious meal with just salted cod, olive oil, garlic and cayenne peppers. Truthful or not, there is no doubt that this is one of the best ways to eat salted cod.

The challenge of this recipe is the sauce. If you think you have mastered the process, you can join one of the many cod in Pil Pil sauce cooking contests that are celebrated across the Basque country every summer.

Preparation

Read the complete recipe first to decide whether to make the sauce whilst the fish is cooking (method 1) or after the fish is cooked (method 2).

De-salting and preparing the fish

If using salt cod then desalt as follows. Wash the fish under cold running water rubbing the outside to remove excess salt. Soak the cod, skin up, in cold water for 48 to 72 hours, changing the water every eight hours. After the cod has been desalted and rehydrated, remove the fish and pat it dry.

You could use fresh cod instead, but make sure to adjust the salt to taste.

Cut larger cod fillets in fist-sized pieces, but not smaller than 10 cm.

Cooking the fish

1. Heat a large frying or sauté pan and pour in the olive oil. Add slices of garlic and dry cayenne pepper. Cook at low temperature until the garlic is lightly brown. Discard the garlic and the cayenne pepper.
2. Lower the temperature of the oil even more and once it has cooled down place all the fish in the pan skin up. The fish should be cooked as "confit", which means slow-cooked in fat. In practice this means that the oil should never get too hot. Cook until the cod is flaky, but do not overcook as it would get too dry. The fish should be juicy and tender.

Making the Pil Pil Sauce

The challenge of this recipe is the sauce, which has to have the consistency of a light mayonnaise. The basic concept is to emulsify the sauce by mixing the fish juice with the olive oil, but it is not always easy. There are many ways to cook the sauce. The traditional way of cooking the Pil Pil sauce is method 1.

Method 1

3a. As you cook the fish, gently move the pan in constant strokes to mix the fish juice with the oil. Bubbles from the juice of the cod will start to form in the oil and, as you shake the pan in constant strokes, the bubbles will become smaller and start mixing with the oil until the sauce reaches the proper consistency.

A ceramic pan works best here. Remember to keep the oil at a very low temperature while cooking.

It takes quite some time, approximately 20 minutes, to cook the sauce, so be patient. This traditional way of cooking the Pil Pil sauce is the most rewarding. However to be able to cook it this way, you need to have a fire/gas stove or an old electrical stove. Be aware that the pan has to be on top of the heat whilst being constantly moved, and rubbing the pan against the cooking surface may damage a modern electric or induction stove. In this case, there is an alternative way that can be used to mix the sauce.

Method 2

3b. Remove the fish from the pan once the juice has come out. Keep the pan on the low heat. Use a metal sieve to emulsify the sauce. With a sieve stir the sauce in fast circular movements to whisk all the ingredients together and make the sauce airy. The secret here is to keep the oil warm: if it becomes too hot, the mixing will not happen as the cod juice will evaporate. The colour of the Pil Pil sauce depends on the quality of the oil, the colour is lighter if the olive oil is refined. Watch a video on how to make the Pil Pil sauce using a sieve https://youtu.be/sp7LffN8OSM?t=75.

Serve cod with the Pil Pil sauce. Decorate the plate with the garlic and the cayenne pepper.

Mustard and Balsamic Chicken and Tomato Traybake with Greens and Broccoli

Jessye Aggleton

MSc in Archaeology
Matriculation: 2011 (Hertford College)
Joined St Cross College: 2014

UK

Serves 2 people

Cooking time: 45 minutes–1 hour

England

Ingredients

4 chicken thighs (skin on, with bone), can use drumsticks too

5 tomatoes

2 cloves garlic

1 heaped teaspoon Dijon mustard

1 teaspoon balsamic vinegar

1 head of spring greens (leaves separated)

½ head of broccoli

Vegetable stock

A dash of dried mixed Italian herbs

Salt and pepper

Since moving to St Cross College accommodation, I have liked the kitchen in our Wellington Square house basement. For the first time away from home I have access to a lot of kitchen space and a proper working oven, so I have learnt to cook a range of adapted and some invented dishes using mostly store cupboard items that do not need much money to buy or many hours to make. The food that I cook is fairly healthy, filling and pretty quick to prepare. This is one of my favourite dinners I have cooked for myself while at St Cross.

Preparation

1. Preheat conventional oven to 200°C, fan oven to 180°C, or gas mark 6.
2. Wash and halve the tomatoes. Arrange the tomatoes flat face up in a large roasting tray, and sprinkle each with a small pinch of salt and pepper.
3. Cut the garlic cloves in halves or quarters.
4. Rinse the chicken under cold running water (be careful not to spray water from the chicken beyond the sink as chicken skin can harbour pathogenic bacteria). Pat dry. Trim any excess fat from the chicken and score two deep marks through the skin into the meat. Push a little garlic into each of the scores.
5. In a separate bowl mix the Dijon mustard and balsamic vinegar together and spread onto each piece of chicken, making sure to also coat the underside.
6. Arrange the chicken skin-side up around the tomatoes in the roasting tray. Pour a glug of balsamic vinegar over the tomatoes, then put the tray in the oven for 35 minutes.

Side meal of boiled greens and broccoli

7. While chicken is in the oven, wash and slice the spring greens roughly into 1 cm long strips, only use the green part. Cut the broccoli into small florets.
8. Preheat the frying pan and add the vegetable stock (about 2.5 cm deep) and allow it to simmer.

9. When there is roughly 20 minutes left on the chicken, put the vegetables into the stock, add the Italian herbs, and allow to simmer. Check the vegetables occasionally to see if they may need more or less heat. If they are cooked before the chicken is ready, take off the heat and put them back on once the chicken is nearly ready.
10. Drain the vegetables, and serve them as a bed to the roast chicken and tomatoes. Drizzle a little liquid from the tray onto the chicken to serve.

Braised Greek Chicken

Tony Hope

Emeritus Fellow in Medical Ethics

UK

Serves 4 people

Preparation 20 minutes, cooking 3-6 hours

Casserole dish

Greece

Ingredients

1 whole chicken

6 prunes (more if no plums)

6 fresh plums (optional). In season replace all prunes by plums

300g cherry tomatoes (or other small variety)

150g mushrooms

1 heaped tablespoon (20ml total) of roughly equal proportions of: cinnamon, nutmeg and cloves

2 teaspoons salt

400–500ml water

Greece must be a popular holiday destination for many Oxford scholars – the history, literature and archaeological sites adding spice to the climate, beauty, and food.

I like to remember holidays through meals. Food can be as good as photos in bringing back to life those times under the sun or stars, or, when less lucky, huddling in a café out of the rain. Holidays can also inspire home cooking: new ingredients, new combinations, new cooking methods.

This recipe takes me straight back to the Greek island, Skopelos, and to a particular restaurant. It was a family holiday and the four of us sat in the warm of the evening under a walnut tree by a small pond. The signature dish of the restaurant was braised chicken. The recipe had been passed to the owner from his mother. You had to order the dish in the morning as the chicken was cooked on a low heat for most of the day. It was served at the table in the pot surrounded by the dark juices, the soft moist meat falling off the bones. We ate and talked and drank the local wine into the evening.

Back home in a colder and wetter Oxford we tried to repeat the experience several times, the dish evolving as season and inclination dictated. When we cooked it one cold September evening we added some 'sweet' spices (cinnamon, nutmeg and cloves) for comfort and by analogy with plum pudding, and have found that this works on hot days as well.

Preparation

1. Soak the prunes if they are very dry. Stone and roughly chop the plums and prunes.
2. Roughly chop the mushrooms.
3. Place chicken in a casserole dish.
4. Add chopped plums, prunes, mushrooms, tomatoes, and spices round the chicken.

5. Add water to come to just less than one third up the sides of the chicken.
6. Bring to the boil on stove and then cover with a lid and put in oven (conventional oven 160°C; 150°C fan; 325°F; regulo 3) and cook for at least 3 hours, or, even better, on slightly lower heat (150°C/ 300°F/ regulo 2) for 6 hours.
7. Serve on a large plate with some of the juices in a jug; or directly from the pot.

Variations

Chopped walnuts can be added (a large handful) as in the original Skopelos dish. Spices can be varied, or omitted, to suit taste. Herbs, such as tarragon or thyme, can be added – best added in the last hour of cooking, but this dish is generous and not fussy, so you don't have to be obsessional.

Braised Whole Pheasant in Red Wine

Anne and Martin Vessey

Martin Vessey, Emeritus Professor of Social and Community Medicine and Emeritus Fellow of St Cross College. Became a Fellow of St Cross College in 1973
Anne Vessey, Martin Vessey's wife.

UK

---

4 servings (one pheasant serves 2 people)

Cooking time: 60-80 minutes (preparation to soften the bird 9-11 hours optional)

Medium or large casserole or deep baking tray with a lid that would fit two pheasant

Oxfordshire, England

Ingredients

Quantities are given for two pheasants

- 2 pheasants (plucked and prepared for cooking by a butcher)
- 2 teaspoons of olive oil
- 1 large onion
- 2 cloves of garlic
- 150g of mushrooms
- 150g tomatoes (6 small tomatoes)
- 1 celery stick
- 250ml of red wine (optional 150ml of red wine and 100ml of water)
- Garlic purée (optional for thickening the sauce)
- ½ teaspoon salt

My wife Anne has often found roast pheasant to be disappointing. The flesh can be difficult to separate, it is easy to overcook or undercook and so on. Using her braised pheasant recipe, consistent results can be obtained and it is easy to separate meat from bone and tendon. Where we live, in the Cotswolds, pheasants are easily obtainable and pretty cheap to buy so it is worth getting the hang of them!

Our first pheasant was given to us about 45 years ago by a delightful chap who ran a small garage in the village we then lived in. One morning he gave Anne a bag saying "I've got exactly what you need Anne – a couple of cocks and a pheasant too". Yes – he was definitely trying to embarrass and tease Anne! There was a lot of wriggling in the bag and when Anne took it home she found it contained two live bantam cocks and a dead pheasant! The cocks, which fought all the time, went in a wire netting cage in the garden for the children but were pretty soon eaten by an enterprising fox which dug under the wire. Anne cooked the pheasant – it was not a success!

Preparation

1. Slice the onion; cut the celery in 1-2cm pieces; chop the garlic; quarter the tomatoes and mushrooms. Set aside.

2. Rinse the pheasants under cold running water. Pat dry with paper towels. Remove any remaining feathers.
3. Heat a casserole dish on the hob on medium-high heat, and add olive oil.
4. Brown a pheasant in the casserole dish for 2-3 minutes on one side until it has taken on some colour. Turn pheasant through 90 degrees and brown for another 2-3 minutes. Turn again through 90 degrees and brown. Finally turn again through 90 degrees and brown, so that all four sides of the bird are browned. You are not cooking the bird at this stage, but giving it a little colour and enhancing the flavour.
5. Remove the pheasant from the casserole dish and set aside on a plate.
6. Repeat this browning process with the second bird. Set the second pheasant aside but leave the casserole pan on the hob and do not clean it since you will cook vegetables in the oil and juices from the birds.
7. Turn down the heat under the casserole dish. Add the onion, celery, garlic, tomatoes and mushrooms. Cook the vegetables for 3-4 minutes to soften them, stirring occasionally. When the vegetables are no longer in danger of burning, put the lid on casserole and keep cooking the vegetables for another 10 min. Check and stir occasionally to prevent burning.
8. Preheat oven to 180°C.
9. Put the pheasants on top of vegetables in the casserole pan. Add the salt and pour the wine over the birds. Add a little garlic puree if desired. Place the lid on the casserole pan and put it on the top shelf of the pre-heated oven. Cook for 45 min.
10. Test that the bird is properly cooked by sticking a skewer or sharp knife into a thick part of the meat. There should be no juice, or if any it should be clear. If there is pink juice, cook for another 10 minutes and test again.

11. Check the sauce: if it needs thickening use the garlic puree or thickening granules. Season with salt to taste. Serve with mashed potatoes, peas and small carrots. The dish can be reheated to eat the following day.

Olena's tips

The recipe was tested and approved by a party of over 15 people at a dinner I cooked for friends at Pusey House. I had to cook about ten pheasants, and although purchased from a local butcher, no bird was like another, some older and some younger. The older birds and those raised more naturally have tougher meat. To achieve consistently soft texture of meat of the cooked game birds, I prepared the pheasants for braising as my mother taught me. Avoid using any strong marinade, as it will reduce the natural flavour of the game meat, instead, do as follows. Rinse a bird under the cold running water. In a large bowl put a bird and pour over enough cold water mixed with the juice of 1/2 a lemon (per bird) to cover the whole bird. Cover the bowl with a lid or cling film. Leave it in a refrigerator for approximately 7-9 hours or overnight. In the morning, discard the water and pat the birds dry. In a small plate combine freshly ground pepper and salt. Rub the mixture over the outside of a pheasant, rub some under the skin where possible. Do not worry about the quantities of salt, the meat will only take as much salt as it needs. Put the birds in a large bowl, cover with cling film, and leave in a refrigerator for 1-2 hours at least, or, ideally, for the rest of the day, and cook in the evening. Cook as described in the recipe above, but do not add any more salt

Chilean Baked Beef Empanadas "Empanadas de Horno"

Ingredients

Filling
- 5 medium onions
- 450 g of lean minced beef
- 1/3 teaspoon ground cumin (or to taste)
- ½ teaspoon ground black pepper
- 1 teaspoon paprika powder
- 1 (not completely full) teaspoon ground oregano
- 1 teaspoon ground coriander
- 4-6 hard-boiled and peeled eggs (1/4 of an egg per empanada)
- Jar of black pitted olives (2 olives per empanada)
- Raisins (optional)
- Dried whole chilli pepper or ground dried chilli flakes (optional)
- Salt to taste
- Vegetable oil

Dough
- 770 g of plain flour
- 1 levelled teaspoon of baking powder
- 30 g of chilled butter (cut into cubes of a medium size)
- 475 ml of hot milk
- Salt (a levelled tablespoon or to taste)

Cindy Santander

DPhil in Zoology
Matriculation: 2014

Chile and the USA

Makes 21 medium or 15 large empanadas. One empanada serves one person.

Preparation:
90-120 minutes. The meat filling has to rest in the fridge for about 12 hours.
Baking: 30-40 mins

Chile

The origin of the Chilean empanada has its roots in the Old World. Prior to the Inquisition, the Moors had left a rich and diverse culinary influence in Spain. Alongside invasion and conquest, the Spanish brought with them their varied gastronomy and introduced empanada to South America. It now stars as a traditional national cuisine found famously in almost all festivities. In particular, the empanada is the main dish of the Independence Day celebrations.

What truly makes the Chilean empanada properly "Chilean" is the authentic filling – pino. Pino is made of a unique combination of spices that creates a distinct flavour different from other empanadas found throughout the Americas. The recipe below is one that comes from my maternal family and it is now my family's way of preparing this much-loved dish.

Preparation

Filling (Pino)

1. Chop the onions into tiny cubes.
2. In a bowl mix onions and minced meat.
3. Heat 2 teaspoons of vegetable oil in a pan, add meat and then spices and salt. Fry at medium heat, stirring occasionally. Cook for about 10-15 minutes. A good pino is cooked until the onions are translucent and there is no meat juice, but the meat should not be overly cooked and slightly pink. Once the meat is cooked, it can be tasted and the quantities of spices and salt adjusted.
4. Remove from the heat, and leave to cool and rest for at least 12 hours in the fridge. By letting pino rest overnight in the fridge you allow the beef to absorb all the flavours from the spices.

Dough (Prepare once the Pino has rested in the fridge)

5. Bring milk close to boiling. Add salt. Add butter cubes one by one, so that the milk does not cool down quickly.
6. In a large bowl mix baking powder and flour.
7. Gradually fold the milk over the flour with a wooden or rubber spatula. Don't use a metal spoon, because the milk is hot. When done correctly, the dough is too hot to touch, but cool enough to be able to hold the bowl for mixing.
8. Using a spatula stir the dough until all the flour is well absorbed by the liquid. The texture should be neither too dry nor too wet – it should stick to your fingers.
9. On a flat floured surface knead the dough. The loose plain flour prevents the dough from sticking to hands and surface. Knead until the dough no longer sticks to your hands, this is a sign that the dough is ready.
10. Put the dough in a bowl and cover it with a moist kitchen towel.

Assembling the pastry

11. Take a few pieces of dough of about the size of a small ball. On a lightly floured flat surface roll out each piece of dough to make a round of about 15-16 cm across and 2-3 mm thick (size of a teacup saucer). The dough should be rolled out finely, but remain firm enough to wrap in a filling. Excess dough can be cut off with a knife and put back in a bowl with the dough for later. Repeat this until the whole dough is used.
12. Drain the olives
13. Cut boiled eggs in quarters lengthwise.
14. Firmly pack a heaped tablespoon of meat filling along the centre of each round, leaving a margin for folding.
15. Place a quarter of an egg on the side of the meat filling and two olives on each side of the meat mound. Raisins could be added as an option, but in our family we would refrain.
16. Seal each empanada by folding one side over the filling and pinching the edges together. The edges would stick better if you pinch them with fingers dipped in cold water. Keep in mind that you should leave enough margin for the edges to be folded inwards.

17. To give empanadas the golden finish, brush them with a mix of egg yolk, a little water and ground paprika. Usually the egg white is conveniently saved to make Pisco Sour, a cocktail that goes well with Chilean empanadas

Baking

18. Preheat the oven to 180°C Fan.
19. Cover a baking tray with an aluminium foil, and sprinkle it with flour to prevent sticking. Place empanadas 5 cm apart from each other. Prick the top of each empanada with a fork.
20. Place a tray in the middle of the oven and bake for 30-40 min. In a gas oven, the baking tray should be placed further away from the hottest site. Empanadas are done when the dough is cooked and golden.

You can go creative with folding empanadas, for example you could do a Cornish pastry fold. Traditionally, Chilean empanadas are folded with three blunt outer edges, two on each side and one in the front. These dough folds taste great when dipped in sauces. In Chile we use pebre and chancho en piedra, or Chilean salsas.

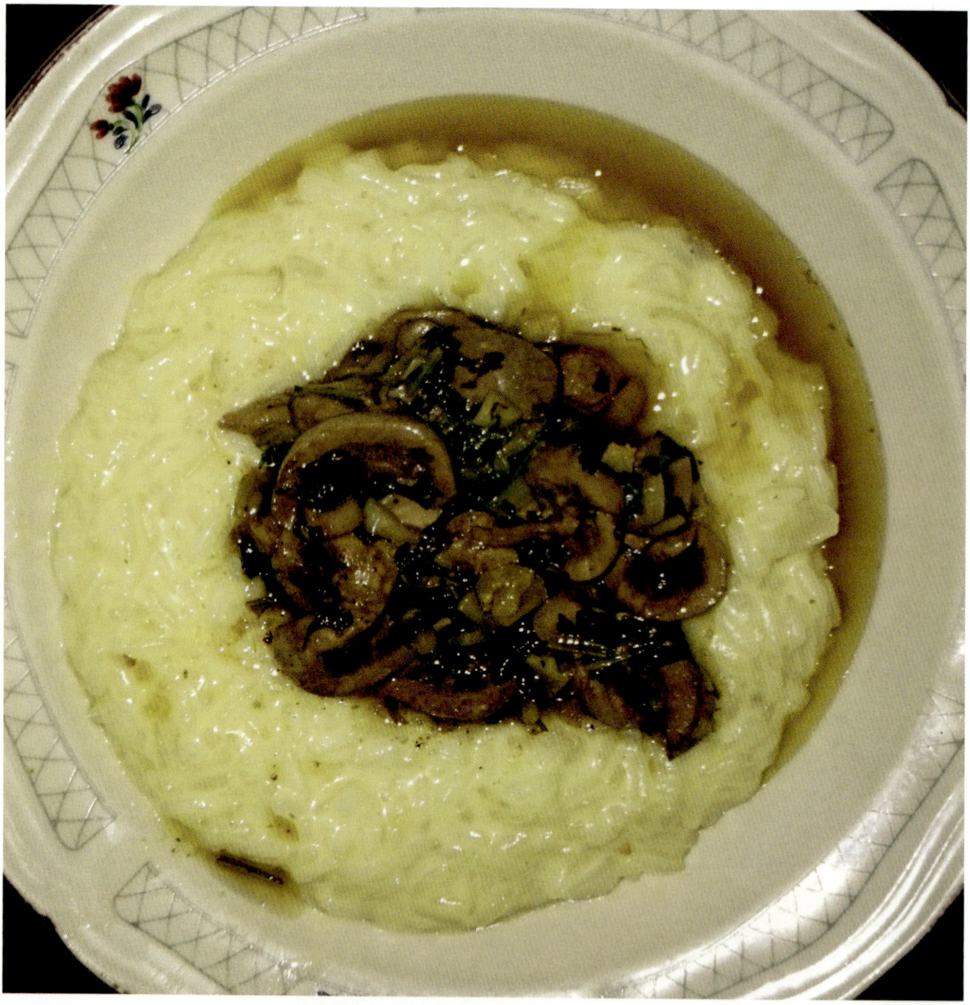

Risotto with Lambs' Kidneys

Preparation

1. Finely chop the onions, garlic and parsley, set aside. You can adjust the quantity of garlic to personal taste.
2. Rinse the lambs' kidneys under cold running water. Pat dry. Cut the kidneys in thin slices, set aside.

Cooking risotto

3. In a large saucepan warm 50 ml olive oil on medium-high heat, stir in the chopped onions and cook till translucent.
4. Add rice and stir until the rice is coated with oil.
5. When the rice has taken on pale gold colour from the oil, pour in wine, stirring constantly until the wine is fully absorbed. Add some freshly ground black pepper.
6. Add one or two ladles of chicken stock at a time, stirring until the stock is absorbed. Continue adding chicken stock as required till the rice is cooked. The rice should be slightly *al dente* (still has a bite, but not hard in the centre). Do not overcook it.
7. Add the parmesan, switch off the heat, and stir well to achieve a creamy texture.
8. Cover with a lid and let the risotto rest.

Cooking lambs' kidneys

9. In a frying pan warm 50ml of the olive oil and the butter on medium-high heat.
10. Add chopped garlic and stir for a minute. Do not cook garlic to brown.
11. Add the sliced lambs' kidneys, cook for 4-5 min. The kidneys should be just cooked through but not overcooked.
12. Add chopped parsley, stir and add a juice of half a lemon or one lime. Add some freshly ground black pepper.

Serving suggestions

Spoon the risotto into warm dishes and top with the lambs' kidneys.

The butter and oil from the lambs' kidneys make the risotto rich and creamy.

Sunil K. Sukumaran

DPhil in Organic Chemistry, Dyson Perrins Laboratory
Matriculation: 1990

India

Serves 5-8 people

Cooking time: 40 minutes-1 hour

India

Ingredients

500g rice (Arborio, Carnaroli, or any small-grained rice)

300g lambs' kidneys

200g grated parmesan

2 medium onions

2 garlic heads

1 large bunch of parsley or coriander (cilantro)

100ml extra-virgin olive oil

50g butter

500-600ml chicken stock

1 glass white wine (or a splash of dry Vermouth)

½ lemon (or 1 lime)

Freshly ground black pepper

Salt to taste

Punjene Paprike (Stuffed Peppers)

Ilija Rašović

DPhil Materials Science
Joined St Cross in 2014.
Matriculated: 2010
(Corpus Christi)

British Citizen

Serves 3-6 depending on how hungry everyone is

Preparation time: 40-50 minutes.
Cooking time: 40-60 minutes

Yugoslavia

Ingredients

4-6 medium size bell peppers
1 cup of rice
1 large onion
4 rashers of smoked bacon
500g minced pork
1 clove of garlic
2-5 mushrooms (optional), amount dependents on how much of a mushroom flavour you want
150g tomato purée
1 can of chopped tomatoes
1 cup of chilled boiled water
1 carrot, grated
1 small courgette or fresh tomatoes, sliced so there is one slice for each pepper
Olive oil
Dry sage
Salt
Black pepper

Stuffed peppers is a staple dish ubiquitous throughout the republics of the former Yugoslavia. The recipe in different variations exists in Bulgaria, Romania, Hungary, Slovakia and the Czech Republic. No doubt, such a wholesome meal can be found beyond these countries too.

This meal brings peacefulness to my world and unites people together. My family are Serbs originating from Hercegovina and Croatia. In spite of the complex situation in that part of the world, food remains a tonic for the soul, and stuffed peppers, or as we call them punjene paprike, are a hearty essential. Its taste brings back to me special childhood memories of visiting family in remote villages, from the mountains of Hercegovina to the vast plain of Vojvodina. Most precious moments were those when family and friends would get together to celebrate Christmases, Easters, weddings and Slave, the feast days of family saints. On those days the songs are sung and rakija flows until the wee hours.

The above recipe comes courtesy of my dear mother. And, of course, it is the best there is. May it bring you as much comfort and joy as it does to me.

Prijatno!

Preparation

1. Wash all the vegetables.
2. Boil rice in salted water for 10 minutes then drain the water. Set aside.
3. While the rice is boiling, finely chop onions, bacon, mushrooms and garlic. Chop canned tomatoes. Grate a carrot. Slice a courgette or fresh tomato. Set aside.
4. With a small knife cut the tops off the peppers, carefully remove the seeds from each pepper and wash off any remaining seeds thoroughly. Set aside.

Cooking

5. Use a pan with high sides. Preheat a pan and add a tablespoon of olive oil. Cook on medium heat. Put the

chopped onion and mushrooms in the pan and cook for 5 minutes. Stir occasionally.

6. Add the chopped bacon, minced pork and garlic. Cook for 10-15 minutes until brown stirring occasionally. Let it simmer on low heat.
7. Add the tomato purée and stir gently and then, in order, stirring gently before adding next ingredient: the canned chopped tomatoes; the cup of chilled boiled water; the grated carrot; and the boiled rice.
8. Season with salt, pepper and sage to taste. Take off the heat.
9. Spoon the mixture into the peppers until fully stuffed.
10. Top each of the peppers with a slice of courgette or tomato.
11. Preheat oven to 180°C.
12. Sprinkle a baking tray with the olive oil. Arrange the stuffed peppers placing them cut sides upwards. Any remaining meat and vegetables stuffing could be spread around the bottom of the baking tray.
13. Cover with foil and cook for 40-60 minutes.

Serving suggestions

Serve with cheesy mashed potatoes.

Olena's tips

For a hearty vegetarian dish, substitute the meat with the mushrooms or minced "Quorn".

To make bell peppers more tender, after cutting off the tops and removing the seeds, place the peppers in a deep saucepan, cut parts facing upwards, and pour freshly boiled water to completely cover the peppers. Cover with a lid and leave for 10-15 minutes.

Moo Gratiem Pork with Garlic

Mary J Warrell

Professor of Vaccinology, Oxford Vaccine Group. Wife of David Warrell, Emeritus Fellow of St Cross

United Kingdom

Serves 3-4 people

Preparation and cooking time: 30-40 minutes, allow at least 1 hour to marinade the meat

Wok

Thailand

Ingredients

- 200-300g pork filet (you can increase the amount but it will take longer to prepare)
- 3 cloves of garlic
- 2 tablespoons Worcestershire sauce
- Black pepper
- 1 tablespoon oil (you might need more)
- 1 tablespoon Fish sauce made in Thailand, not squid origin
- ½ tablespoon vinegar
- 1 level tablespoon sugar
- Bird's-eye red chillies (use to make sauce, optional)

I learned about Thai cooking by watching my cook, Biak, in a small steam filled kitchen in Bangkok. David and I went there at the start of the Wellcome-Mahidol University of Oxford Tropical Medicine Research Unit in 1979. This was the origin of the current Tropical Medicine Network widespread in Asia and Africa, based in the Nuffield Department of Clinical Medicine.

Having maids was an unexpected marvellous benefit of living in Thailand, especially later on when we had two young children. The city has become radically modernised since then. Food was normally bought in local markets. American food could be found at small supermarkets with limited varying stocks. I 'treated' the weevils resident in an expensive pack of cornflakes by heating in the oven. Clearly not long enough, as on opening the door a cloud of tiny insects flew out.

Several of the cooking ingredients used are not easily available if at all in the UK. I adapt recipes to local produce and family taste.

Preparation

1. Peel and finely chop garlic.
2. In a large bowl mix garlic with two tablespoons of Worcester sauce and grind in lots of black pepper.
3. Slice pork into thin smallish pieces (about 1 cm×4 cm) and thoroughly mix into the marinade. Add more sauce to saturate and more pepper.
4. Leave covered at room temperature for an hour or more. If preparing ahead put into a fridge. Mix again before cooking.
5. Heat 1 tablespoon of oil in a wok. Add small amount of meat and quickly lay pieces flat in a single layer. Cook over a low heat, shaking the wok occasionally. After about 2 minutes, when one side begins to brown, turn over to briefly finish cooking.
6. Remove meat from the wok, put aside and cook the remainder in batches, adding oil between batches as needed.

7. When cooking the final batch of meat, add in the marinade, fish sauce, vinegar, sugar and 2 tablespoons of water.
8. Return all meat to the wok, mix thoroughly, warm through and taste to check the vinegar and sugar seasoning.
9. Put into serving dish. Clean wok with little water and add residue to the dish.

Serving suggestions

Serve with a steaming Thai jasmine rice and a chilli fish sauce on the side.

To make the sauce. Deseed and chop fine the bird's-eye red chillies. Mix the chillies with approximately two tablespoons of fish sauce. Moo gratiem should be one of several dishes shared at a meal.

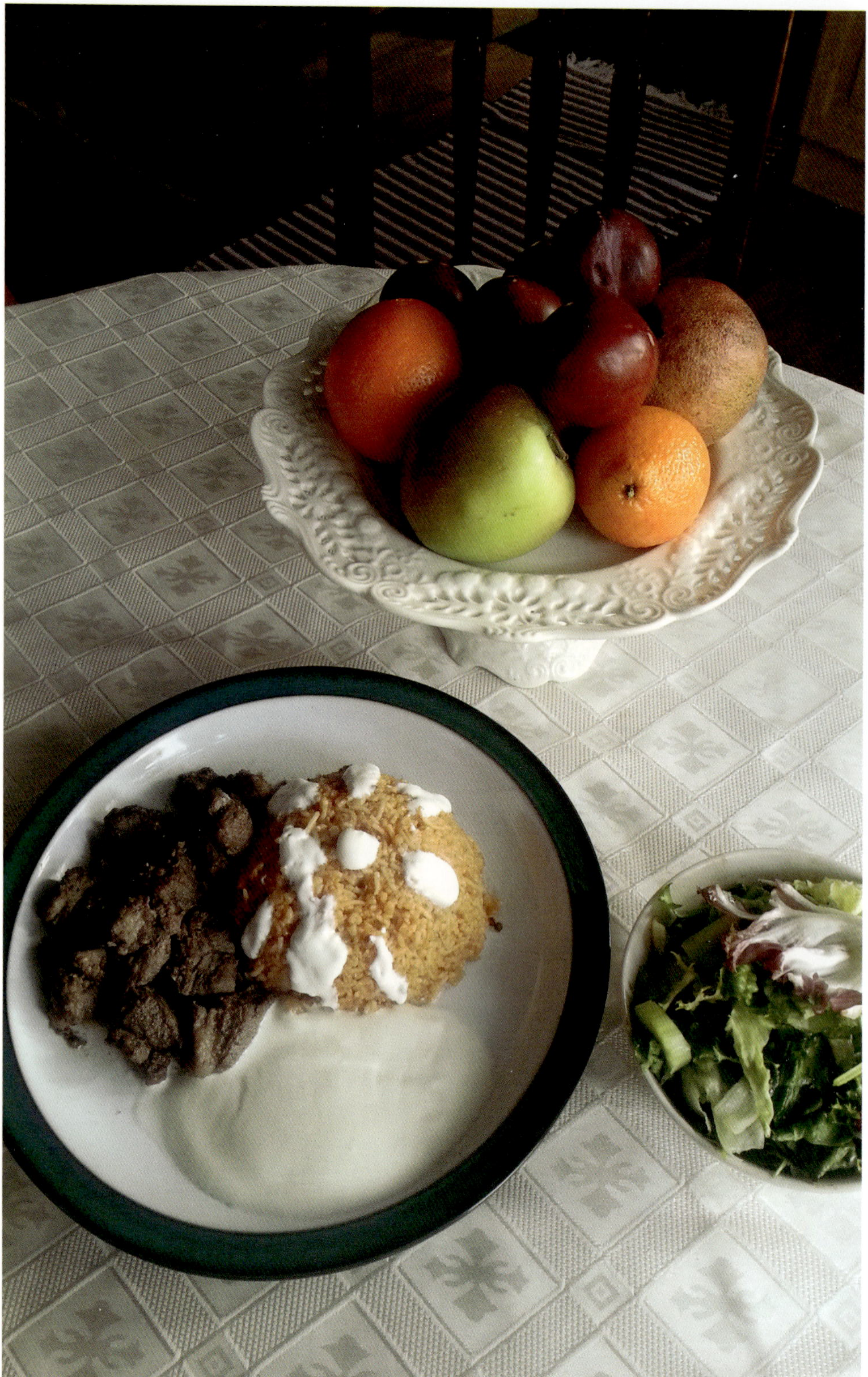

Afelia

Sophia Toumazou

DPhil in Zoology
Matriculation: 2013

UK

Serves 3-4 people

Cooking time:
45 minutes; preparation:
1-9 hours to marinate the pork

Cyprus

Ingredients

500g of diced pork shoulder

1 glass of dry red wine

3 tablespoons of crushed coriander seeds

4-5 tablespoons of olive oil

Salt to taste

Afelia is a traditional pork dish from the island of Cyprus. Its aromatic combination of red wine and coriander seeds truly represents the heart of Greek Cypriot cuisine and the passion that is invested in such home-made dishes. It is a very easy dish to make that only requires your keen eye to watch over the pork as it stews and sucks in all the juices and flavours of the red wine and coriander admixture. This recipe goes back generations in my family and each mouthful of the succulent pork reminds me of the days when I was very young visiting my grandmother in the village during the hot summers, being surrounded by my extended Greek family and sitting round the table to eat good, simple and tasty Cypriot food. Of course, nothing beats the quality of Greek olive oil that is a key ingredient in making this wonderful dish.

Preparation

1. Put the pork in a bowl with the wine, coriander and a sprinkle of salt. Leave to marinate for at least one to two hours. For a richer taste, leave to marinate over night in the fridge.
2. Heat the olive oil in a large pan. Place all of the meat and its marinade into the pan.
3. Stir regularly, cover and simmer for 40 minutes on low heat or until the pork is tender. If the pork is still not tender then add half a cup of water and a bit more wine so it can cook for longer. Add salt to taste.
4. Serve with pourgouri (see recipe: *Pourgouri pilaf*), plain Greek yoghurt and a salad.

This recipe is in memory of my late mother, Niki Tyrimou-Toumazou, who taught me that good food is the heart of any home and any family. I hope you enjoy making this as much as my mother did and I hope you enjoy eating it as much I did.

Galapagos Seafood Rice

Anthony Geffen

Fellow by Special Election
CEO & Executive Producer, Atlantic Productions Ltd.

UK

Serves 6 to 8 people

Preparation time: 15 minutes and cooking time: 1 hour

Two saucepans, one medium and one large

Galapagos

Ingredients

2 tablespoons oil

2 tablespoons white onion, finely chopped

1 garlic clove, minced

2 cups long grain rice

2 ¼ cups fish stock

3 tablespoons sunflower, peanut or light olive oil

1 ½ cup white onion, finely chopped

2 heads garlic, peeled and crushed

1 red bell pepper, diced

1 ½ teaspoons cumin

1 teaspoon achiote (annatto) powder

1 bunch of coriander, finely chopped

1.8 kg seafood, such as a mixture of some or all of the following: prawns, squid strips, scallops, mussels, clams, crab and whitefish fillets (cut in bite-sized pieces)

Salt and pepper

Two hundred years after Charles Darwin set foot on the shores of Galapagos Island, David Attenborough and I made a three part series on this wild and mysterious archipelago. These extraordinary ever changing islands have given birth to species and subspecies that exist nowhere else in the world.

While we were filming we saw the discovery of a new species, a pink Iguana but we also witnessed the end of a species as we were the last people to film the famous Pinta Tortoise, Lonesome George before he died.

Galapagos is one of the most extraordinary places I have visited, and while we were on the island David and I discovered a dish we enjoyed on several occasions, a seafood rice dish. Below is the recipe.

Antony Geffen received his first of two BAFTA awards for the documentary about Galapagos wild life.

Preparation

1. In a smaller saucepan heat the first measure of oil (2 tablespoons) over a medium flame and add the onion and garlic. Keep stirring until the onion is translucent.
2. Add the rice and stir until each grain is coated in oil.
3. Add the fish stock and bring to a boil.
4. Continue to boil until the fish stock is absorbed, then reduce the heat as low as it will go. Cover the pot and let it simmer for 15 minutes, or until the rice is al-dente, when the grains are soft but still have a slight crunch when you bite.
5. In a larger saucepan heat the second measure of oil (3 tablespoons) and add the rest of the chopped onions, and then two whole heads of crushed garlic. Cook until the onions are translucent.
6. Add the spices, half of the coriander and the bell pepper. Cook for 5 more minutes stirring throughout.
7. Add the seafood in order of how long it will take each to cook (white fish, the shellfish and the large prawns first). Cook the white fish and large prawns for 3 min stir frequently, add the rest of the seafood and keep stirring for another 3-4 minutes.
8. Transfer the rice to the saucepan and mix well. Keep stirring for another minute or so, or until everything is cooked through.
9. Add the rest of the coriander, salt and pepper to taste.

Loin of Venison with a Sloe Gin and Blackberry Glaze, and Smoked Mash

(The College 50th anniversary dinner main)

St Cross Catering Team

UK

Serves 6 people

Cooking time: 40 minutes–1 hour

Ovenproof frying pan
(Potato ricer)
(Fine-meshed drum sieve)

United Kingdom

Ingredients

For the roast venison and glaze
- 1 kg venison loin
- 1 tablespoon rapeseed (or olive) oil
- 1 tablespoon dried thyme
- 1 tablespoon vegetable oil
- 2 tablespoons sloe gin
- 200 ml beef stock (good quality from supermarket)
- 6 juniper berries
- 200 g blackberries
- Knob of butter
- Salt and pepper

For the smoked mash
- 1 kg charlotte potatoes
- 1 tablespoon salt
- 300 g cold smoked butter, cut into cubes (you may need to look online for a source of smoked butter. Smoking your own requires special equipment).
- Warm milk, to taste

Preparation

Venison and glaze

1. Trim any fat from the venison. Rub with the rapeseed oil, dried thyme, salt & pepper.
2. Heat vegetable oil in an ovenproof frying pan and seal the venison, browning on all sides.
3. Place the pan with the venison in oven for 6-8 minutes or until the venison is cooked but still pink inside. Cook for longer if you prefer the meat less pink. Remove the meat from the pan after cooking and set aside.
4. Pour the sloe gin into the pan used to cook the venison and cook till the liquid is reduced by half. Add the stock and the juniper, reduce by half again.
5. Strain the sauce and return it to the pan, add the blackberries and cook for 2 mins till the blackberries have softened.
6. Add the butter to the sauce and check the seasoning.
7. Cut the loin into 3 thick pieces per person and serve with the sloe gin glaze on top.

Smoked mash

1. Peel the potatoes and cut them into 2.5 cm slices. Run the slices under cold water to wash off surface starch.
2. Heat a large pan of water until it reaches a temperature of 80°C/175°F (you'll need to use a good-quality heat thermometer, with the probe placed in the water).
3. Add the potatoes and simmer for half an hour being careful to maintain the temperature at 70°C/160°F.
4. Drain the potato slices and run them under cold water until completely cool.
5. Rinse the pan and refill with cold water. Salt the water and bring it to the boil, then lower to a simmer.
6. Add the cooked, cooled potatoes and cook until soft.
7. Drain the potatoes, then place them back in the pan. Shake the pan over a gentle heat to get rid of any remaining water.
8. Tip the potatoes into a ricer and rice the potatoes over a bowl containing the cold smoked butter (or mash potatoes and butter thoroughly with a fork). Push the buttery riced potatoes through a fine-meshed drum sieve (or other sieve) for a silky, light texture. You can prepare the purée in advance up to this stage and store it in the fridge.
9. To serve, reheat the purée gently in a pan, while gradually whisking in a little warm milk.

Haggis, Neeps and Tatties

(Burns' night main)

St Cross Catering Team

UK

Serves 6 people

Cooking time: 2-3 hours

Scotland

Ingredients

1.2-1.5 kg haggis (meat, or vegetarian according to your preference)

600 g potatoes, peeled and roughly chopped

600 g turnips, peeled, roughly chopped

A generous pinch of grated nutmeg

4 tablespoons milk

4 tablespoons butter

Sea salt and pepper

Preparation

Haggis

1. Follow the cooking instructions on your shop-bought haggis carefully. Cooking times vary.

   For the haggis we use we first place it in a large pot and cover with cold water. We then cover the pan with a lid, bring to the boil, then reduce to a simmer and cook for 40 minutes per 450 g.

Tatties (potatoes)

2. Place the potatoes in a large saucepan, cover with cold water, add a pinch of salt, cover the pan with a lid. Bring the potatoes to the boil, reduce to a simmer and cook until tender (approximately 20 minutes).
3. Drain the potatoes and keep to one side.
4. Add half of the butter and half the milk to the pan the potatoes were cooked in. Melt the butter and warm the milk, add the cooked potatoes and mash.
5. Add the nutmeg and stir well to create a smooth, creamy mash

Neeps (turnips)

6. Place the turnips in a large saucepan, cover with cold water, add a pinch of salt, cover the pan with a lid. Bring the turnips to the boil, reduce to a simmer and cook until tender (approximately 20 minutes).
7. Drain the turnips and keep to one side. Add half of the butter and half the milk to the pan the turnips were cooked in. Melt the butter and warm the milk, add the cooked turnips and mash.

Serving

Once cooked, remove the haggis from the water. Place on a serving dish and cut it open with scissors or a knife and serve with the tatties and neeps.

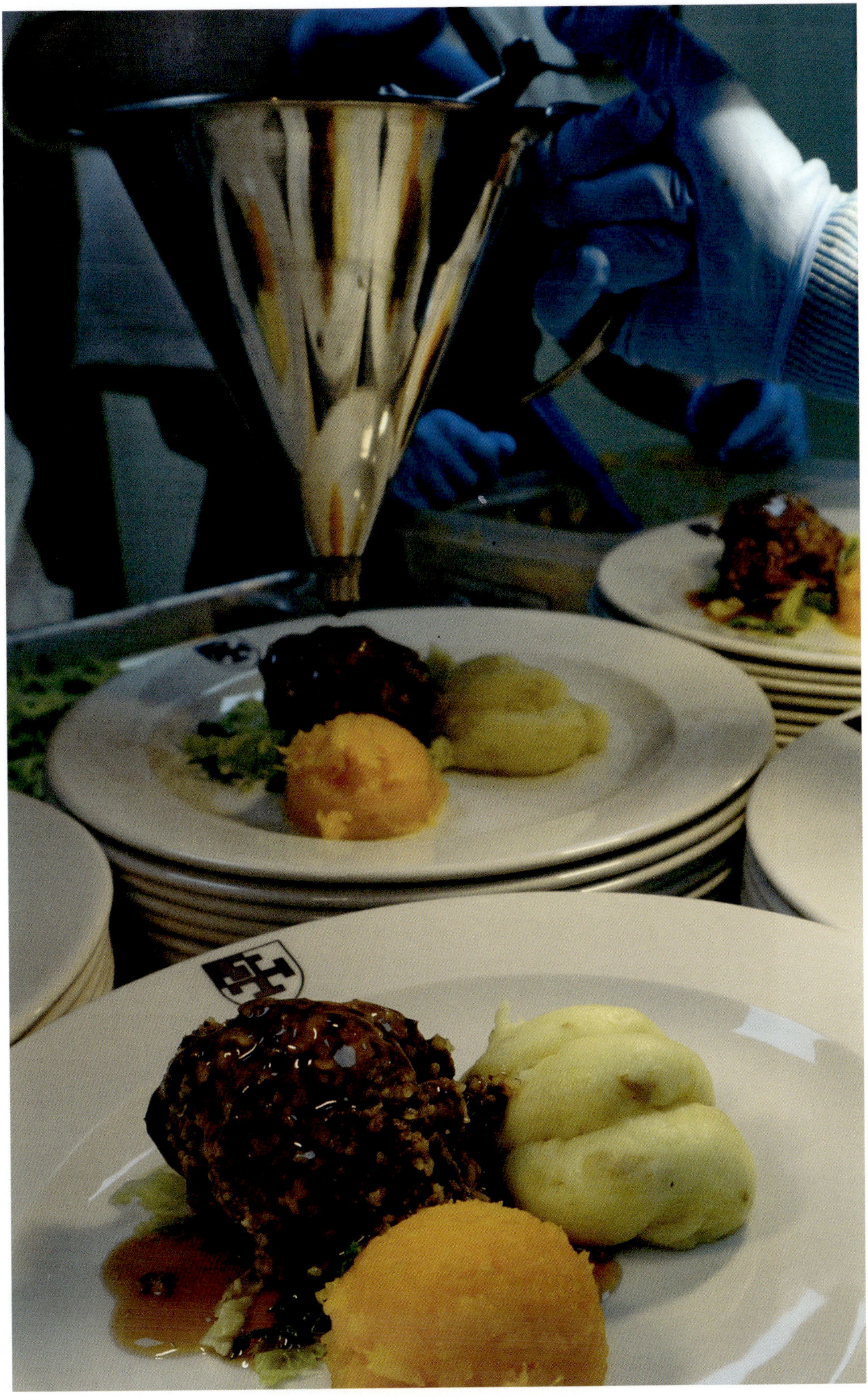

Japanese Curry and Rice

Takuya Okada

Oxford Uehiro–St Cross Scholar 2014-2015

Japan

Serves 2 people

Cooking time: 20-40 minutes

Rice cooker (optional)

Japan

Ingredients

1 potato

1 carrot

½ onion

Meat (4 rashers of bacon or any other meat)

2 pieces of Japanese curry roux (available online and in oriental shops – choose any you like)

160 g rice

Although sushi is perhaps the most famous Japanese food, few Japanese people cook sushi. The traditional "mum's food" in Japan is Japanese curry rice. I usually find cooking troublesome and, with the wonderful lunch at St Cross College, do not often feel like cooking. But when I feel that I would like to have something with a Japanese touch, I cook this curry rice. What is good about the curry is that you can put in whatever you like, such as an egg or an aubergine in addition to the ingredients in the original recipe, just as you might do with a soup. Thus, the curry and rice can be quite nutritious, and, at the same time, you can use up the leftovers from the refrigerator. Moreover, it is said that the taste soaks into the curry over time, so you can cook a larger batch of curry and leave it in the fridge for a few days. Japanese curry rice is thus a good choice for a lazy cook like me or for students busy studying.

Preparation

1. In a pan pour enough water to cover the potato and bring to the boil.
2. Meanwhile peel and dice the potato. Rinse under cold running water to wash off the starch.
3. When the water is boiling add cut potato into the pan.
4. Dice the carrot, onion, and meat. Add one after the other into the pan as you go. The water should remain boiling all the time.
5. Reduce the heat, add the curry roux to the stew, stir, and then simmer for around 15 minutes. If you find there is too little water, add more water to get the consistency of a curry that you prefer.
6. While the curry is simmering, cook the rice.
7. Put rice in the bowl and add the curry on top, serve hot.

Desserts & Drinks

Vlokken Cake – Dutch Cake with Chocolate Flakes

Wybo Weirsma

DPhil in Information, Communication and the Social Sciences
Matriculation: 2012

The Netherlands

Serves 8-10 people

20-40 minutes preparation and assembling and 130 minutes baking time

A mixer and baking paper

The Netherlands

Ingredients

5 eggs
300-350 g caster sugar
Oil or butter for baking
500-600 ml double or whipping cream
1 pack of 'Vlokken', chocolate flakes or chocolate sprinkles

Vlokken (Dutch for flakes) cake is an utterly Dutch cake. The traditional recipe is calling for the cake decoration with uniquely shaped chocolate flakes: 'Vlokken'. Since these are only available in the Netherlands, if you are elsewhere in the world use any chocolate flakes or sprinkles you can find. Besides being Dutch, it is a family recipe as well. And there is no reference to it online. My father used to make this cake for our birthdays every year when we were kids.

My father is no longer with us, but we continue the family tradition, and now I make the cake. Having made it for my birthday several times, I can confirm that while the cake is easy to make, it tastes delicious. Moreover, all the ingredients, except for the 'Vlokken', are easy to find and do not cost much. Thus, it is a perfect birthday cake for a busy Oxford student.

Preparation

1. Separate the egg whites from the yolks. No traces of yolks should enter a bowl with the egg whites, or they will not whisk into a stiff foam.
2. With a motor or hand mixer whisk the egg whites until so firm that if you turn the bowl upside down, the mixture will not fall out.
3. Gradually mix in the sugar. Do not add all the sugar at once.
4. Cut off two roughly square pieces of baking paper of the same size. Grease each on one side with a little oil or butter.
5. On each sheet of the baking paper, with a spoon or spatula, distribute equal amounts of the whipped egg whites to make two similar circles about 2 cm thick.
6. Preheat the oven to 100°C. Bake at low heat for 130 minutes.
7. Remove the meringue (the baked egg white) from the oven once done (a few brown patches and soft spots are normal).

8. In a bowl whip the cream until stiff.
9. Thoroughly spread a little over a half of the whipped cream on the bottom meringue and cover it with the second meringue. Distribute the rest of the whipped cream on top and on the sides.
10. Sprinkle the cake with 'Vlokken' or chocolate flakes until only a little cream shows.

Since it is an ultimate birthday cake, do not forget to sing the "Happy Birthday" song when serving it

Olena's tips

If you are not able to find the Dutch chocolate 'Vlokken' or quality chocolate sprinkles, buy a bar of good dark chocolate, and grate it using a cheese grater. Use to decorate the cake.

The Oxford Graduate Students' Tiramisu

Irene Milana

MPhil in Modern Japanese Studies
Matriculation: 2013

Italy

Serves 5-6 people

Preparation:
30-40 minutes and refrigerate for 2 hours before serving

Italy

Ingredients

6 eggs
500 g mascarpone cheese
100-120 g sugar
Pack of "Lady Finger" biscuits (simple rich tea biscuits could be a substitute)
Strong coffee

No oven in your accommodation? Housemates stressed out by deadlines and exams? Did you leave the table a mess and you want to make it up to them for cleaning it up?

I found out during my time at Oxford that no homemade dessert has the same cheering effect as a good tiramisu. I got my housemates to vacuum clean, buy groceries and make me litres of tea by only mentioning it. You should definitely give it a try, it seriously is the best recipe to make people happy, and it's so easy everyone will think you are as good as our College chef Rob. You just need very fresh eggs, mascarpone cheese and a strong wrist to whip it all up.

If coffee is not your thing, as if that was even possible, the tiramisu tastes marvelous with berries. Just heat up your favourite berries with a bit of water, sugar and lemon juice, let it dry and then use it instead of the coffee for dipping the biscuits.

Preparation

1. Make a good amount of coffee and let it cool down. You could always drink any coffee leftover.
2. Separate the yolks from the whites of the eggs.
3. Mix the yolks and the sugar until all the sugar is dissolved, the yolks are pale and the mixture is fluffy. Gently fold in the mascarpone cheese, mix it all well together until smooth.
4. In a clean bowl whisk the egg whites until they form stiff peaks.
6. Gently combine together the yolks mixture and the whipped egg whites, mixing throughout to achieve the airy texture of a mousse.
7. Use a large bowl or container (use glasses if you want to make individual portions), dip the biscuits in the coffee and place them at the bottom of the bowl, spoon and

smooth a layer of the 'mousse' on top of biscuits. Alternate a layer of biscuits and mousse.

8. Put the tiramisu in the fridge for two hours to set.
9. Before serving decorate with cocoa and pieces of chocolate on the top.

Olena's tips

Another variation of the classic dessert is the green tea tiramisu. I discovered this new and extremely tasty variation of tiramisu in a small Japanese-French fusion restaurant in Nice, where we went together with colleagues from Oxford after presenting at the conference. To make green tea tiramisu, dilute Matcha green tea powder in hot water, in proportion 1 teaspoon per 150 ml. Add more tea powder for stronger flavour. Let the tea cool, and then dip the biscuits. Make about 300-400 ml of Matcha green tea for the quantities provided in the recipe. If it is not enough, you can always make more Matcha green tea. Prepare the mousse as described above.

Caramel Squares

Rosa von Gleichen

DPhil in Social Policy
Matriculation: 2014

United States of America

Serves 10 people and more

Preparation time
10-15 minutes, baking time
30 minutes, and 2 hours
to cool before serving

Great Britain

Ingredients

To make shortbread
150g plain flour
45g caster sugar
100g unsalted butter

To make caramel
320g condensed milk (a little less than 1 tin)
1.5 tablespoons golden syrup (makes caramel more firm) or honey (less firm)
50g caster sugar
100g unsalted butter
100g milk chocolate

As the English love biscuits and I love to bake, the thought of learning to bake an English biscuit during my time at Oxford came naturally and early. But which of the thousand types sold in little bakeries around Oxford was I to master? After sacrificing a balanced diet by "tasting" several kinds of biscuits a day, I happened upon the caramel square, also known as millionaire's shortbread. Though originally Scottish, shortbread is an essential British biscuit, topped with caramel and chocolate – a clear winner.

My first attempts were quite feeble (dough without eggs?), and my dear St Crossers would nobly and obligingly eat overly crumbly or sweet batches and give me input. There was also an unfortunate incident at my home in Cowley, where I employed the help of my windowsill to make the squares cool faster, which ended in accidental defenestration. But by the end of Michaelmas I'm proud to say, I was finally able to produce delicious caramel squares that brought a sweetened finish to coffee in the lounge after lunch at St Cross. In many ways, this particular caramel square is now an authentic St Cross biscuit, as a group of us created it and continue to enjoy it.

Preparation

Shortbread

1. Pre-heat oven to 200°C.
2. Melt the butter in a pan on a low heat – don't cook or burn it.
3. Mix the flour and caster sugar in a bowl.
4. Pour in the melted butter.
5. Knead the mixture together until it forms a dough.
6. Press the dough into the base of the greased tin.
7. Prick the dough lightly with a fork in several places.
8. Bake in the pre-heated oven for 30 mins or until firm to the touch and very lightly browned. Allow to cool in the tin.

Caramel

9. When the shortbread is nearly done, pour the condensed milk, syrup, sugar and butter into a saucepan.
10. Cook over a low heat, then steadily increasing heat, stirring all the time (best use a mixer to avoid clumps). Watch it closely, take off the heat when the colour turns deep caramel, and pour over the shortbread.

Finish

11. Melt chocolate and pour it on top of caramel.
12. Let it cool for 1 hour at room temperature and 1 hour in fridge, until chocolate is so firm it cracks when you cut.
13. Cut into squares.

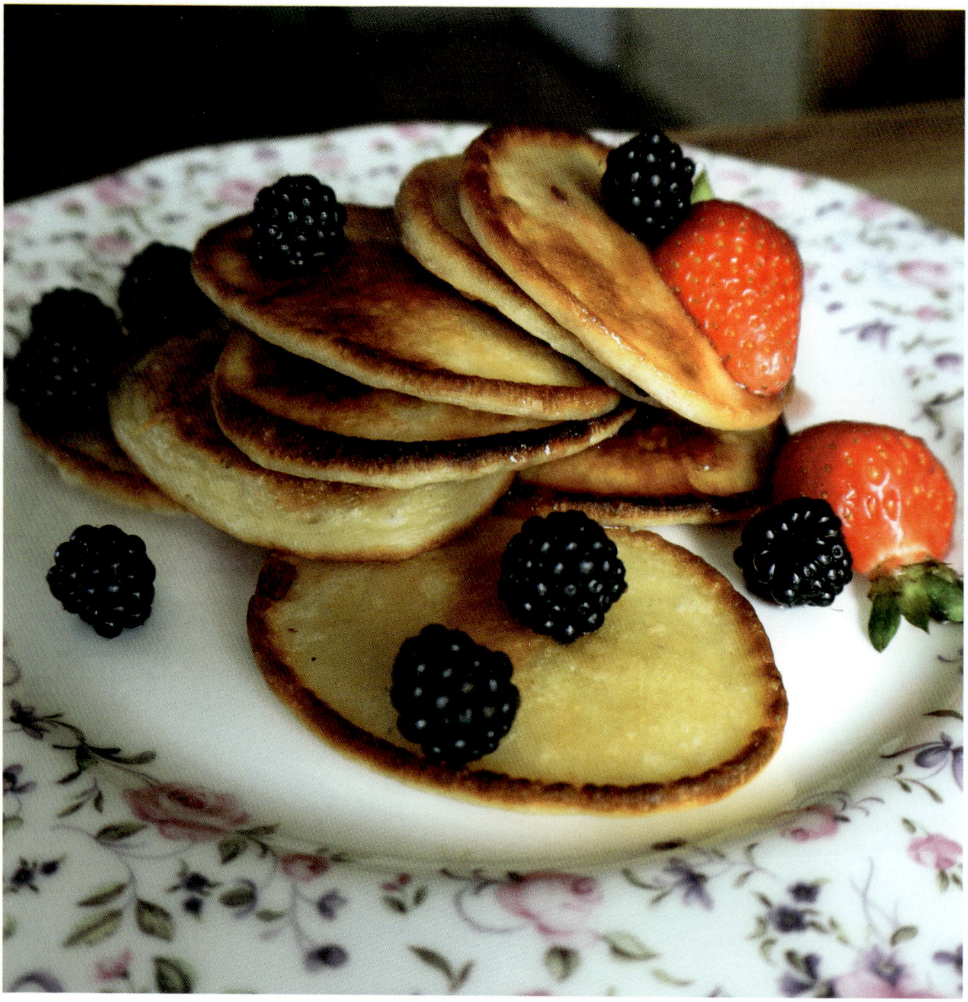

Oatmeal and Yogurt Pancakes

Preparation

1. Cook the oats with water, as you would do for a thick porridge. Remove from the heat and allow to cool slightly; if used hot it will cook the egg.
2. In a smaller bowl mix together the dry ingredients: flour, salt and baking soda.
3. Make batter in a large bowl by beating the egg, and then mixing in yogurt and cooked oats. Stir well until combined. Add in the flour mixture, a little at a time, and beat until combined.
4. Preheat and butter the pan, use just enough butter and oil to prevent sticking, add more if required between the batches of pancakes.
5. Using a large spoon or a ladle pour batter into the pan and cook on a medium heat. Flip the pancakes over when they seem dry around the edges, and the surface is covered in small bubbles.
6. Serve hot with Maple syrup on top.

Ethan Sherr-Ziarko

DPhil in General Linguistics
Matriculation: 2011

United States of America

Enough for 3

Cooking time: 20-30 minutes.

United States of America

Ingredients

230 g plain or vanilla yogurt
100 g flour
45 g rolled oats
2 g salt
1 egg
4 g baking soda
Butter
Cooking oil
Maple syrup, Grade A or B (optional)

Mom's Melting Shortbread

Rhea Sookdeosingh (recipe of my mother Lillian Norma Sookdeosingh)

DPhil in History
Matriculation: 2014

Canada

Serves 10 people and more (the recipe yields approximately 5 dozen biscuits)

30 minutes preparation and 25 minutes baking

Canada

Ingredients
3 cups flour
½ cup cornflour
1 cup icing sugar
450g unsalted butter

For me, these melting shortbread cookies conjure the happiest childhood memories. Along with sparkling snow (the beauty of which never lasts, as anyone from a snowy climate knows too well) and the smell of pine and clementines, my mother's cookies are synonymous with Christmas – with family, fireplaces, food, and all the joys of the festive season.

Though my sister and I loved the Christmas season for many reasons, we especially welcomed December's opportunity to gorge ourselves on these cookies, above all other treats. As it happened, the recipe was lost during our adolescence, and though shortbread cookies abound, I knew of no one else who made these particular Melting Shortbread cookies. So many years passed with no sightings of Santa, and no Melting Shortbread.

The recipe was eventually recovered, to our immense delight. It was found in time for my mother to send me these wonderful memories of home during my first Christmas in London when I was alone and living in a Harry Potter-esque cupboard under the stairs. My first year at Oxford, and at St Cross, has been a dream come true in many ways. Having moved out of my broom closet into a proper apartment, complete with kitchen, I relished the opportunity to try my hand at these cookies. Though I can't say they're as good as my mother's, it's been a pleasure to bring this happy part of my past into my present. And what a present, indeed.

Preparation

1. With a mixer, cream the butter, add icing sugar – work together thoroughly until creamy.
2. Sift flour and cornflour. With a mixer, add to creamed butter mixture.
3. Flour your hands and scoop out enough mixture for one cookie. Roll it into a ball. Place on ungreased baking sheet. With a floured fork, press lightly to flatten into cookie shape, about 2-3 cm thick.

4. Preheat the oven to 160°C. Place the cookies in the oven and bake until golden brown, approximately 15-25 mins.

The recipe yields approximately 5 dozen cookies. According to my mother, they keep well if you can hide them!

Apfel Strudel – Apple Strudel

Orly Amali

MSc in Social Anthropology
Matriculation: 1998

Israel

Serves 5-8 people

Cooking time:
1 hour-1 hour 30 minutes

Germany

Ingredients

4 apples – Granny Smith or other sweet-sour baking apples, known as 'cooking apples' in the UK (such as Bramleys)

1-4 tablespoons of organic cane sugar

50-100g of raisins or dried blueberries

1 pack puff pastry

1-2 teaspoons of cinnamon powder

3-4 cinnamon sticks

caster sugar or sugar powder (icing sugar)

'To talk about food and cooking is to talk about the dignity of daily life' (The Gaza Kitchen, 2012)

I am in my home, dividing parsley for an upcoming performance-lecture, while the war continues not far from me, and even more strongly some 60 kilometers south of my home.

How do artists respond to such a situation? How can I show my solidarity with the women and men of Gaza from Tel-Aviv? How can I inspire others to practise the muscle of empathy as a political act of solidarity and resistance?

The recipes I chose to share with my St Cross fellows represent a cultural act of disobedience. Firstly, because as a Jewish-Israeli I am not supposed to be cooking Palestinian food, especially not as a way to connect to Gazan women when their homes are being demolished and their lives in threat. Secondly, because my origins go back to Europe, my cultural heritage is supposed to be manifested in my cooking more prominently. Thirdly, as my interpretation of women's actions in the kitchen as a political act of self-liberation and engagement is not a common assumption yet.

What if we can mix flour with gesture, movement of the hand with the feeling we have when we are happy, political concepts with sea salt, what if out of this batter a new dish will be created, a new menu?

In the last years these recipes appear in my performances where I combine cooking with dance. In my performances by showing the process of making food, I give political meaning to many of the unpaid, unnoticed work that people – mainly women – do, in order for our lives to be as comfortable and effortless as they are, or desired, by many in highly-industrialized societies.

The Apfel Strudel is my personal interpretation of a traditional cake that is part of the German culture my grandparents brought with them to Israel. I used to bake this cake for my grandmother every week in her last years.

Where possible, I prefer to buy organic local apples, as sometimes the merchants are the farmers that picked the apples. Ask them which apples are the best for baking; it is their expertise, they know.

Preparation

1. Peel apples and cut them into cubes 1 cm × 2 cm.
2. In a bowl, mix apples with sugar, raisins and cinnamon powder. Begin by adding half the amount you think is needed of sugar and cinnamon powder, taste and add more according to personal taste. The mixture should be sweet yet slightly sour.
3. Sprinkle the flour on a clean, dry surface; unpack the dough, if not rolled, roll it to ½ cm thick making a square of 25-30 cm × 45 cm.
4. Place the filling in the centre of the dough. Spread the filling evenly leaving the edges free on all sides.
5. Fold over the side edge of the dough that is close to you to cover the filling, and then roll the strudel away from you.
6. When rolled, press on the edges of the dough to close the seam.
7. Wrap up the side edges of the dough like a candy wrap, and cut the excess dough.
8. Cover a baking tray with a sheet of baking paper and carefully place the strudel seam-side down in the middle of it.
9. With a sharp knife make 3-4 cuts about 2 cm each in the dough, and insert cinnamon sticks in them.
10. Bake in a preheated oven at 180-190°C for 25-35 minutes.
11. Remove from the oven and let it cool down.
12. Once warm or cool sprinkle the top with the sugar powder.

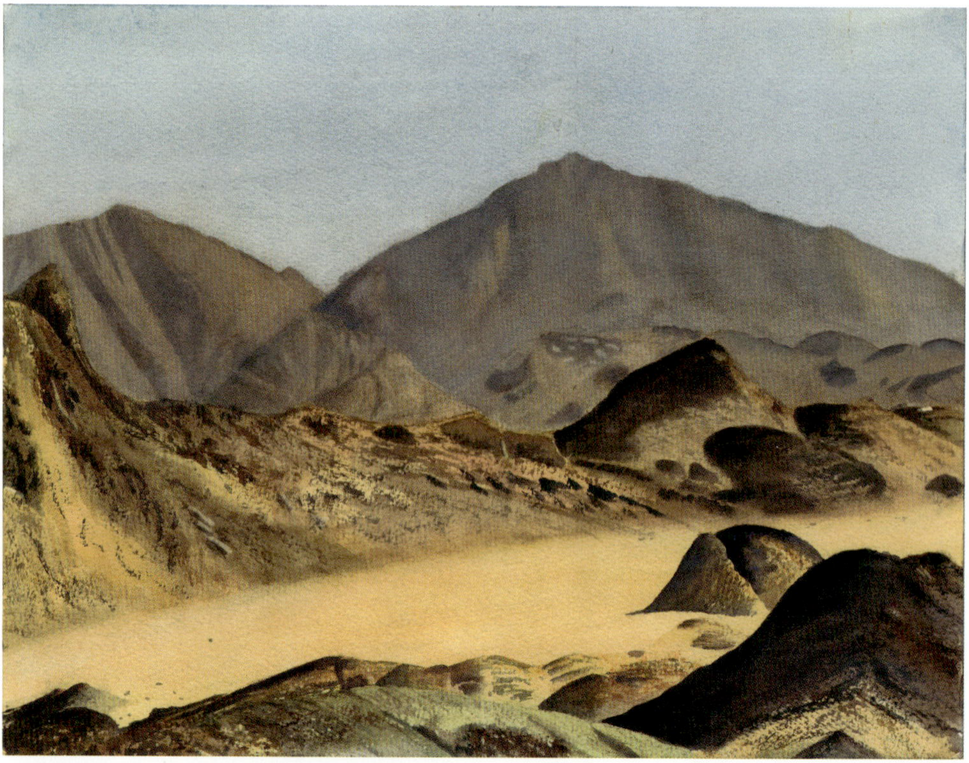

Apple Crumble

The recipe is one that my wife and I developed by experiment from our knowledge of apple crumbles. It is one that I use regularly for our supper as I now have time to cook in retirement. I enjoy it so much I have it at least 3 times a week for supper. It is very easy to make and only takes about 15 minutes to get it into the oven.

E. Christopher Emerson

Barclays Visiting Fellow in 1978-1979

England

Serves 4-6 people

15 minutes to make and 25 minutes to bake

Mixer or mixing bowl

England

Ingredients

200g flour
30g oats
150g chilled butter
2 tablespoons of brown sugar
750g apples (e.g. about 5 Granny Smith apples)

Preparation

1. Wash and dry the apples.
2. Core and peel the apples, then cut each into 8 pieces.
3. Place the apples in an ovenproof dish.
4. Add flour, oats, butter and brown sugar to a food processor, and run it for about 2 minutes, until all the ingredients look well blended.
5. Preheat the oven (170°C degrees in a fan oven or 200°C in a conventional oven).
6. Spread the crumble mixture over the apples until no apple shows. Firm it with a dry knife.
7. Place the dish into the centre of the heated oven and bake for about 25 minutes – until brown on top.
8. Remove from the oven, and once cool enjoy.

Keep the remaining crumble mix for another crumble in the fridge.

Olena's tips

So called 'cooking apples', such as Bramley or Arthur Turner, can be used and have a very fine flavour. For more spicy flavour, after you cut the apples, sprinkle them with two tablespoons of brown sugar and ½ teaspoon of cinnamon and toss.

Venezuelan Rum Cake "Bienmesabe"

Lorena Zuliani-Alvarez

DPhil in Musculoskeletal Sciences
Matriculation: 2012

Venezuela

Serves 10 people

Cooking time:
1 hour 30 minutes

Round cake tin 25 cm in diameter
Trifle dish approximately 25 cm in diameter
Food thermometer

Venezuela

Ingredients

For the sponge
 5 eggs
 250 g caster sugar
 1 teaspoon of vanilla extract
 250 g of self-raising flour
 150 ml good quality dark rum (can be replaced by brandy or sweet sherry)
 Butter to grease the baking tin

For the coconut cream
 300 g of caster sugar
 200 ml of water
 Pinch of salt
 12 egg yolks
 800 ml of coconut milk

For the meringue
 4 egg whites
 100 g of caster sugar

For the topping
 Cinnamon powder (as much as the personal taste requires)

Nothing else brings back memories of the tropical sun of Venezuela in the same way as bienmesabe. The name of this traditional Venezuelan dessert translates "it tastes well". Bienmesabe is a light sponge cake bathed in the Venezuelan rum layered with a sweet coconut cream, and finished with the meringue and cinnamon. This dessert represents the richness of the Venezuelan history and culture. It combines the sponge cake brought by the Spaniards during the colonization with the flavours of the Caribbean coast – coconut and rum.

It's a very popular dessert in the country usually prepared for the family gatherings and celebrations. The most popular recipe of bienmesabe is from an Afro-Venezuelan woman known as Contemplacion. In Caracas, people used to say that the cake she makes has the magic qualities and whoever ate it felt their troubles went away. Here in Oxford, I like to make the cake using her recipe for my friends and co-workers at the university. They all come from different parts of the world, but their common verdict after having a slice of the cake, is that every bite transfers you to the warm Caribbean shores. The taste of bienmesabe can brighten up the grey rainy days that we often have in the UK. I hope this recipe will bring joy and warmth to all those who will try a slice of it.

Preparation

Sponge

1. Preheat the oven to 180°C.
2. Take five eggs. Carefully separate egg yolks from egg whites between two clean dry bowls. Avoid the egg yolks leaking into the egg whites. The latter do not beat up well if the traces of the yolks are present.
3. Whisk the egg yolks, sugar and vanilla extract until pale and thick.
4. Whisk the egg whites until stiff peaks are formed.
5. Using a spatula gently, to prevent the cream from collapsing, fold the whipped egg whites into the egg yolks.
6. Very gently gradually fold the flour into the egg mixture until all is incorporated. Keep the batter airy.

7. Grease a cake tin and pour in the batter.
8. Bake for 35 minutes. Check if the sponge is ready by pushing a toothpick or a skewer through the cake: if it comes out clean, it is ready. If it comes out with bits of the inside of the cake, return to oven and test again a few minutes later. When ready, take sponge out of oven and let cool to room temperature.

Coconut cream

9. While the sponge is in the oven, in a saucepan add the water, sugar and a pinch of salt. Cook on a medium heat, stirring, until the mixture forms a sticky syrup. Remove from heat.
10. In a separate bowl mix well the egg yolks. Add the coconut milk and mix well together until it forms a light cream.
11. In a bowl combine the hot syrup with the egg mixture, whisking quickly as you pour.
12. Transfer to the saucepan in which you prepared the syrup, and return to the stove.
13. Cook the cream on a medium to low heat, stirring constantly until the cream mixture starts to thicken and come to a boil. Remove from the heat and let cool before assembling the cake.

Assembling the cake

14. Slice the sponge horizontally in 1 cm layers.
15. Place the first layer of the sponge at the bottom of a trifle dish, using a pastry brush to moist the sponge with rum.
16. Cover the sponge with the coconut cream.
17. Continue assembling alternating layers of a sponge, rum and cream. Finish with a layer of sponge.
18. Top the cake with the meringue. To make the meringue: in a bowl whisk the egg whites until they form soft peaks. Add the sugar in batches and continue whisking until it forms stiff peaks.

    Place the bowl over a saucepan filled with simmering water. Whisk fast and continuously until a thermometer shows 60°C. Remove from heat and beat until lukewarm and the meringue is stiff. With a spatula spread the meringue evenly on the top of the cake.
19. A final touch is to sprinkle with the cinnamon powder to taste.

Olena's tips

If you prefer the meringue to be a little cooked before eating then finish the cake by placing in a hot oven (200°C) for a few minutes to brown the top of the meringue.

Robin Gaze's Chocolate and Chestnut Log

Tony Hope

Emeritus Fellow in Medical Ethics

UK

Serves 6-8 people

Preparation: 20 minutes. Cooling in fridge: 5 hours

1 lb loaf tin (or any lined container that can go in the fridge)

UK

Ingredients

4 oz (110g) unsalted butter (preferably at room temperature)

4 oz (110g) castor sugar

1 tin (about 1 lb or 450g) Chestnut puree

8 oz (225 g) melted plain chocolate

5 drops Vanilla essence

2 tablespoons rum or brandy

For topping

Whisked double or whipping cream, or almond flakes or summer berries or any combination according to taste

Robinetta (known as Robin) Armfelt studied English literature at Leeds University where she came to know Mary Ogilvie, then Dean of Women's studies. Mary Ogilvie moved to Oxford on being appointed Principal of St Anne's College in 1953. Her brother-in-law, the Anglo-Irish novelist Joyce Cary, was, by this time, a widower living in Parks Road, Oxford (the commemorative blue plaque can be seen on his house opposite the University Parks). Robin moved to Oxford and became Cary's housekeeper and cook. At the end of the dinner parties, Robin would be invited to talk with the guests: people such as Isaiah Berlin, Alan Bullock, Lord David Cecil, Iris Murdoch and Helen Gardner.

Robin moved to Edinburgh to take up a post as Warden of a hostel for girls. At the Edinburgh University Ladies' Tea Club she met a young, suave, lecturer, Mike Gaze, who had completed his doctorate in physiology at Oxford. They married in 1957. Mike was head-hunted by the Nobel Laureate, and Oxford alumnus, Peter Medawar to lead a division in nerve development at The National Institute for Medical Research in London. In 1973 I became one of Mike's doctoral students. I could not have had a better supervisor. Not only did he teach me how to do research but he also invited me back to his house on many occasions where I enjoyed Robin's outstanding cooking. She introduced me to one of those flavour combinations 'made in heaven': chocolate and chestnut. This is her recipe.

Preparation

1. Grease (with butter or oil) the 1lb loaf tin and line with grease-proof paper or parchment.
2. Break up the chocolate and put in heatproof bowl over hot water in a pan to melt.

3. Meanwhile cream butter and sugar together in a large bowl (e.g. by stirring vigorously with a wooden spoon) until the mixture is homogeneous and almost white.

4. Mash the chestnut purée into the creamed mixture, and add the vanilla essence, alcohol and melted chocolate. Mix well

5. Put the mixture into the lined loaf tin and chill in refrigerator for 5 hours [can be frozen and rethawed].

6. Turn out on a pretty plate and decorate with cream or almonds or fresh Summer fruits depending on personal preference

Note: You can make a vegan variant of this using vegetable oil, rather than butter, and vegan chocolate. This pudding is gluten-free.

Fig and Hazelnut Frangipane Tart

(The College 50th anniversary dinner dessert)

St Cross Catering Team

United Kingdom

Serves 6 people

Cooking time: 2 hours

6 × 10cm round loose base tart cases with deep sides (or a single 23cm round loose base tart tin with deep sides)

United Kingdom

Ingredients

For the pastry
 125g cold butter
 250g plain flour
 1 egg

For the frangipane
 225g butter, softened
 1 vanilla pod, split and the seeds scraped out.
 225g caster sugar
 5 eggs
 225g ground almonds
 75g hazelnuts

4 fresh figs

Preparation

For the pastry (or you can buy good quality ready-made butter pastry)

1. Make the pastry by blending butter and flour in a food mixer until it resembles a breadcrumb texture.
2. Add the egg and mix until a firm dough. Wrap in cling wrap and place in a fridge for half an hour.
3. Work on a floured surface and roll out the pastry until about 3mm thick.
4. Line the tart cases with the pastry making sure to press into the edges.
5. Place back in the fridge for 15 minutes.

For the frangipane

6. With an electric hand mixer beat the butter, sugar and vanilla until pale and fluffy
7. Add the eggs one at a time and mix after each addition.
8. Finely chop the hazelnuts and fold them, and the ground almonds, into the mix.

Assembling

9. Preheat the oven to 160°C.
10. Remove pastry from the fridge and spoon the frangipane mix into the tart.
11. Slice the figs in half from top to bottom and add them flesh side up on top of the tart mix.
12. Bake in the preheated oven for 25-30 minutes or until the tart filling has risen and looks golden brown.

Serve warm with either ice cream or whipped cream.

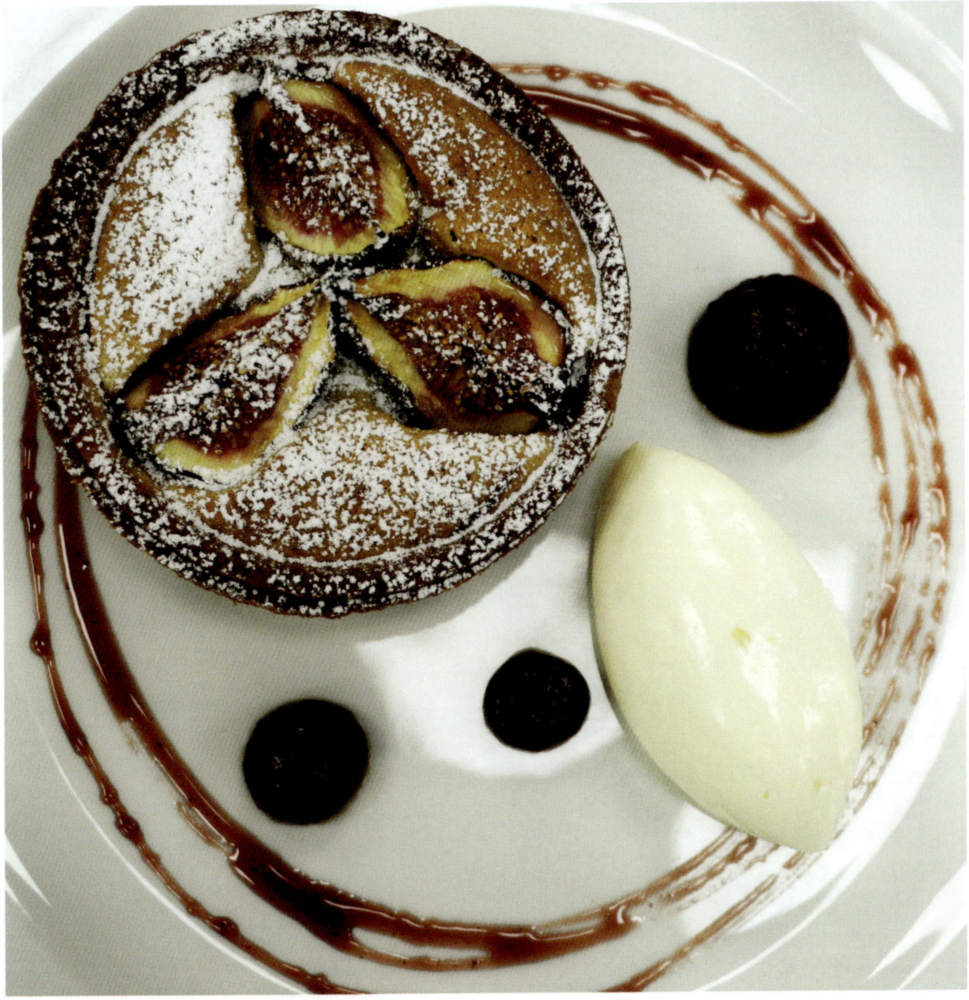

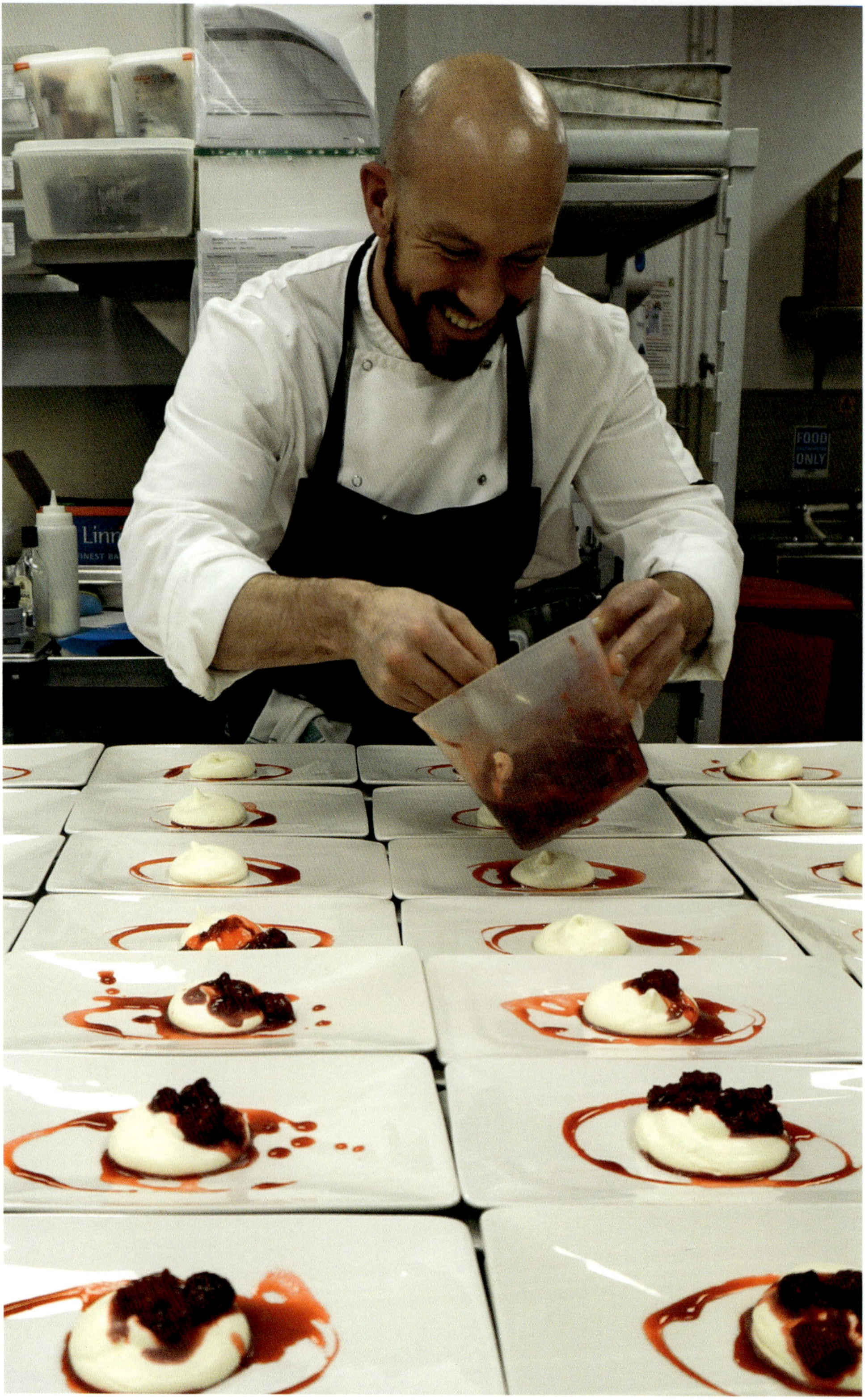
FOOD
ONLY

Cranachan

(Burns' night dessert)

Preparation

1. Toast the oats in a frying pan, being careful not to burn them.
2. Lightly whip the cream until it reaches the soft peak stage, then fold in the whisky, honey, oatmeal and raspberries.
3. Serve in dessert glasses garnished with a few raspberries and mint.

St Cross Catering Team

UK

Serves 6 people

Cooking time: 30 minutes

Scotland

Ingredients

570 ml double cream
85 g porridge oats
7 tablespoons whisky
3 tablespoons honey
450 g raspberries
fresh mint, to garnish

Fruit Smoothie

Lana Pasic

MPhil Development Studies
Matriculation: 2011

Bosnia and Herzegovina

Serves 1-2 people

Preparation time: 15 minutes

Blender

Taiwan

Ingredients

1 medium banana
½ pineapple
1 kiwi
1 teaspoon of flax seeds
½ cup of milk, soya milk or water

The fruit smoothie is a perfect healthy snack to start a day. It can also be a great energy booster and a refreshing summer drink. The idea for this recipe was born when I went travelling after graduating from Oxford. I visited a friend in Taiwan, and every morning in Taipei, she would prepare a refreshing fruit juice.

When I returned home, I cleaned the dust off my blender and decided to make my own version, with one main ingredient – banana, and varying other types of fruit every day. Banana is a great source of magnesium, gives you energy and is a perfect mood-booster. I have been sharing a recipe for this delicious healthy drink ever since. My favourite variation is a pineapple-kiwi mix. Add flax seeds for a boost of omega-3 in your smoothie. I hope that you will enjoy it as much as I do.

Preparation

1. Cut a half of a pineapple, peel it and cut into cubes, or use cubed canned pineapples.
2. Peel the kiwi and cut in quarters.
3. Peel the banana and cut into large pieces.
4. Place the pineapple, kiwi and banana in a blender and add one teaspoon of flax seeds, whole or ground.
5. Add half a cup of water, milk or soya milk, depending on preferences, before blending.
6. Run the blender on a medium speed for about 1-2 minutes until you have the smooth, liquid consistency.
7. Pour into glasses. Decorate with a piece of pineapple, serve with a straw.

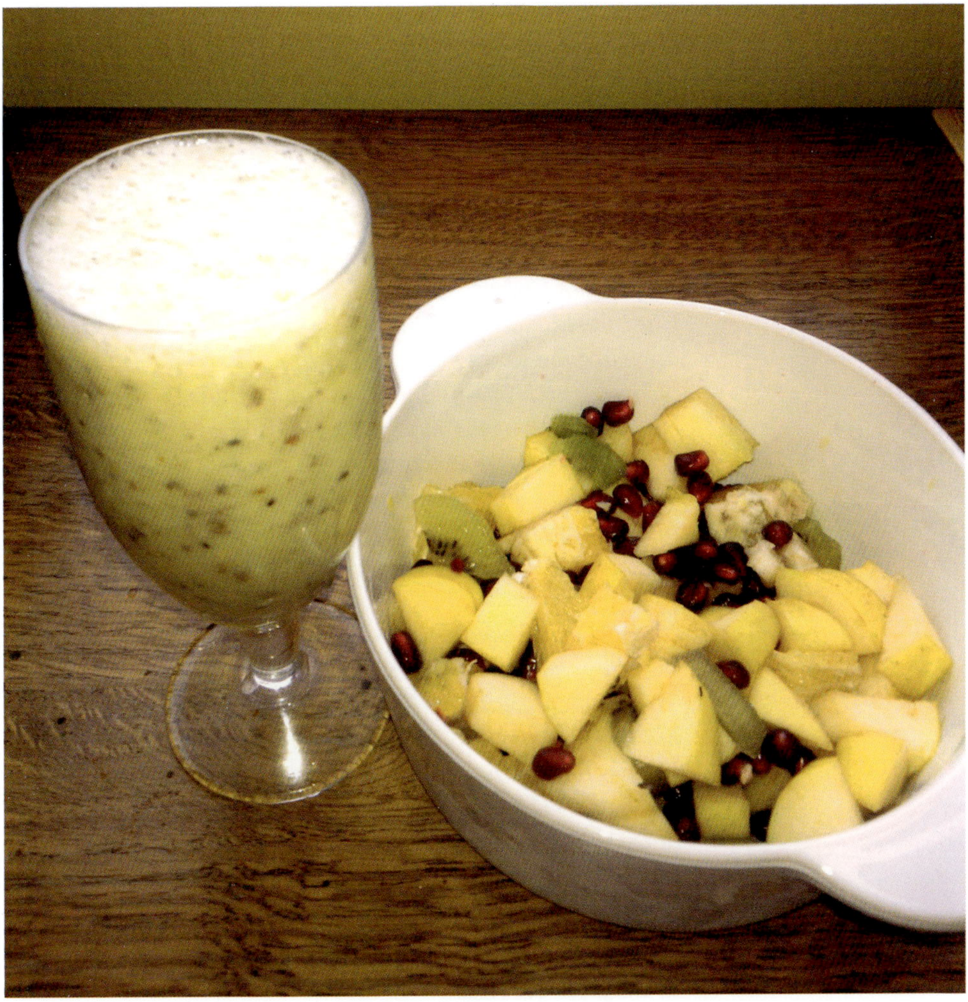

Bloody Charles House Cocktail

Sam V. Aldred

Sacristan of Pusey House
MPhil Candidate in Ecclesiastical History, Keble College, Oxford
Matriculation: 2006

United Kingdom

Serves 1 person

Preparation time: 6 minutes

England

Ingredients

2 measures of vodka (one measure equals 25 ml)
1 measure of port
½ lemon, juice only
Worcestershire sauce
Tabasco sauce
150 ml tomato juice
Horseradish root
Ice cubes

This hard-hitting cocktail is a modification of the much loved Bloody Mary.

It may come as a surprise to some to find that King Charles I of England is regarded as a saint by the Church of England. Yet 'it is as natural', said John Keble, preaching before the University of Oxford, 'that the Church of England should keep this day [January 30th – the date of Charles' death] as it is that Christ's Universal Church should keep St. Stephen's martyrdom.' Many have argued that Charles died to preserve episcopacy in the Church of England and thus kept it to be more clearly a part of the Universal Church, rather than just another Protestant sect. He faced his death with dignity and courage. Famously, as he prepared to step outside to the execution block, he put on a second shirt so that the crowds would not mistake his shivering for fear.

Charles was beheaded that cold winter morning in Westminster as the crowds watched on in horror. The moment that the King's head was severed from his body devout onlookers rushed forward to dip handkerchiefs in his blood, to preserve them as relics. As the Royal Martyr's body was carried to its final resting place at St George's Chapel, Windsor Castle, it is said that a sudden snowstorm caused the black pall over the coffin to be turned white – the colour of purity.

Preparation

1. In a serving glass pour two measures of vodka over the ice cubes, add Worcestershire and Tabasco sauce, then add the port. Use as much Tabasco and Worcestershire sauce as personal taste requires.
2. In a separate cup mix the lemon juice and tomato juice.
3. Pour the tomato juice mixture into a glass with vodka and port. Stir well to blend.
4. Grate a bit of the horseradish root on top to form a white pall of about one 'grating' thick.

Eggs 'n' Baker

Jonathan Baker SSC became Principal of Pusey House in 2003. Bishop Jonathan was the architect, along with Professor Goudie, of the new agreement with St Cross College which ushered in a warm and friendly relationship between House and College. A well-known 'secret' about Bishop Jonathan is that he is ovophobic: that is to say, he has an irrational fear of eggs. This egg-sour cocktail plays off this amusing quirk.

Preparation

In a cocktail shaker mix well whisky, lemon juice and egg white. Present in a tumbler with ice and lemon.

Sam V. Aldred

Sacristan of Pusey House
MPhil Candidate in Ecclesiastical History, Keble College, Oxford
Matriculation: 2006

United Kingdom

Quantities provided for one glass

Preparation time: 6 minutes

Cocktail shaker

England

Ingredients

2 measures of whisky (one measure equals 25 ml)
1 measure of lemon juice
1 egg white
Ice cubes

St Cross College 50th Anniversary Dinner
Saturday 3rd October 2015

This anniversary dinner was served 50 years and two days after the official founding of St Cross College. The reasons why Oxford needed new graduate colleges go back to the time of the First World War. Until then an 'Oxford education' was almost synonymous with a deep grounding in the classics: Greek and Latin literature, history and philosophy. The War had brought to the fore the importance of science and Oxford responded with rapid growth in research in many areas of scientific study. In 1917 British universities decided to introduce for the first time the research doctorate degree (PhD) that had been pioneered in Germany and developed in the US and Canada. Oxford was the first British university to institute this degree calling it the DPhil. The introduction of this degree greatly boosted graduate study and research across the University, not only in the physical and biological sciences but also in the arts and social sciences. Many of these academic areas of study were pursued only at postgraduate level.

The tradition in Oxford, and in the few other collegiate universities, is that all students and all academic staff are not only involved in the relevant faculty of the university but are also members of a college – each college being a multi-disciplinary academic community. By the 1960s, however, fewer than 60% of senior academics in Oxford were members of a college. The traditional colleges, focussed on the needs of undergraduates and their teachers, could not absorb these senior academics particularly as most worked in areas of study that were not part of any undergraduate curriculum. Furthermore, these traditional colleges were finding it difficult to absorb the increasing numbers of graduate students and to cater for their needs as well as the needs of their undergraduates. It was for these reasons that St Cross College was founded on October 1st 1965. In its first year there were 45 Fellows and five students. There are now over 150 fellows and almost 600 students the majority of whom are from outside the UK.

The name 'St Cross' comes from the College's original site in St Cross Road (where the College still has graduate accommodation). In 1980 the College moved to its present site right in the heart of Oxford.

Grand dinners in the UK, until the increased globalisation of the last thirty years, were always French. The College's first major feast, on 9th December 1965 had a rather different menu from this 50th anniversary dinner. It consisted of: truite fumée; consommé julienne; poulet sauté à la crême; mousse de marrons; diables à cheval; dessert; and café. Sherry, a white Burgundy, a claret, port, madeira and a Barsac sweet wine were served at various stages through the meal.

Starter

Seared King Scallops, Charred Onion and Chicken Vinaigrette, Caramelised Onion Purée, Tempura Shallot Rings and Pea Shoots

(see page 34)

Main

Loin of Venison in a Sloe Gin and Home Picked Blackberry Glaze, Smoked Mash and Wilted Greens

(see page 84)

Dessert

Fig and Hazelnut Frangipane Tart with Spicy Wine Syrup

(see page 108)

Traditional Burns' Night Dinner

Burns' Night is a celebration of Robert Burns' life and poetry, and of everything Scottish. It is celebrated on the day of the poet's birthday, January 25. The night starts with a piper piping in guests and ends with the ceilidh dancing. During the night there is plenty of Scottish whisky, good food, kilts and the recitations of Burns' poems. There is a traditional set of courses served on the night. Although some variations are allowed for the starter and the dessert, the main course is always the Haggis. Before the main course is served the host recites "Address to a Haggis" by Robert Burns. Then the Haggis is cut and served. The occasion is one of the most memorable dinners on the College social calendar.

All recipes for the Burns' Night Dinner and the 50th Anniversary of St Cross College Dinner were provided by the St Cross Catering Team (see Acknowledgements).

A typical St Cross Burns' Night three-course dinner is as below, with some good whisky to extend the occasion well into the night.

Starter

Cock-a-Leekie Soup

(see page 36)

Main

Haggis, Neeps and Tatties

(see page 86)

Dessert

Cranachan

(see page 111)

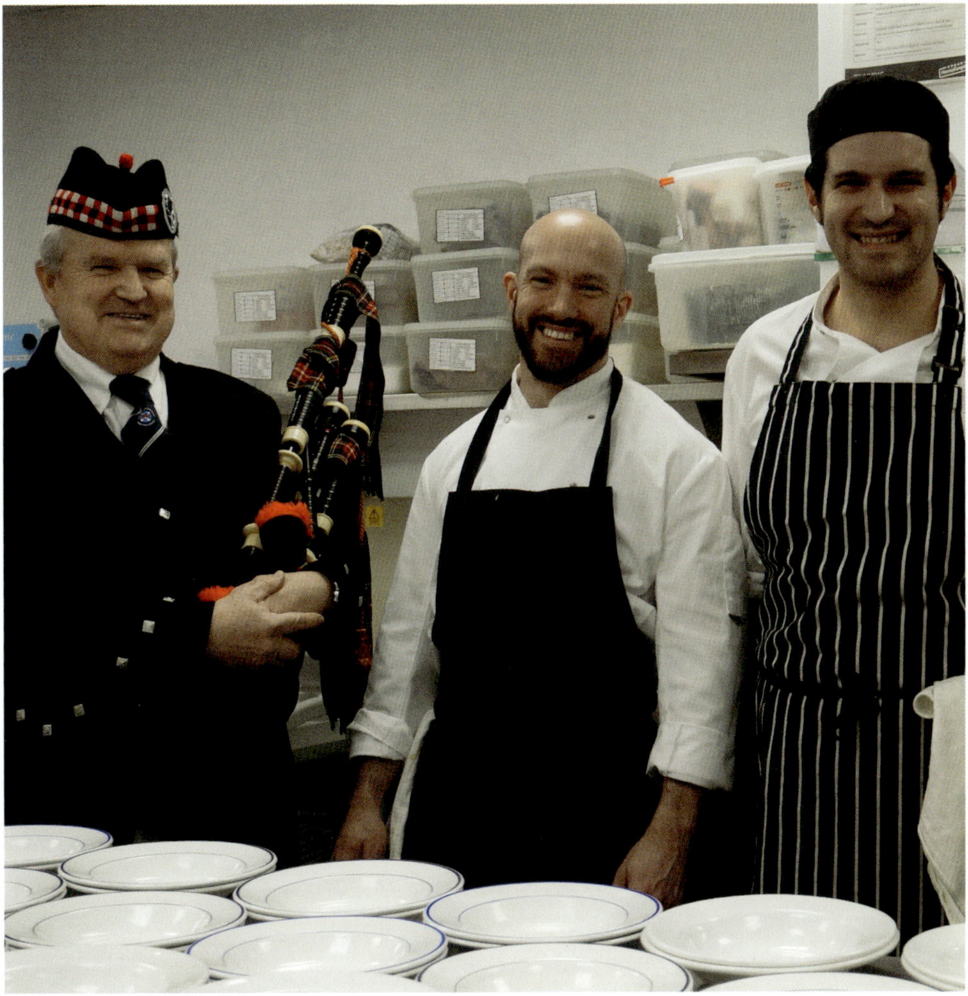

First published in 2017 by St Cross College, University of Oxford

Recipes: © 2017 the respective contributors
Foreword: © 2017 Carole Souter
Remaining text: © 2017 Olena Seminog

Photographs:
The photographs on the recipe pages were kindly provided by the recipe authors except for the pages as specified below.
Olena Seminog: 7, 11, 17, 20, 25, 26, 33, 37, 38, 41, 43, 45, 57, 61, 66, 69, 70, 79, 87, 89, 91, 96, 97, 110, 111, 118, 119
St Cross Catering Team: 35, 85, 109
Atlantic Productions: 82
Jessye Aggleton: 3
Coco Duivenvoorde: 101
Sally Hope: 55, 103, 107, back cover
Haarala Hamilton: Front cover
St Cross College (photographer: David Fisher): Front cover, 1, 2, 9, 14, 19, 40, 93, 115, 117
St Cross College (photographer: Richard Budd): 4, 5, 10, 39, 116
St Cross College: 6

All rights reserved. No parts of this publication may be reproduced, stored in a retrieval system or transmitted, in any form or by any means, without prior permission of the publishers.

St Cross College
61 St Giles
Oxford
OX1 3LZ

www.stx.ox.ac.uk

A catalogue record for this book is available from the British Library

ISBN: 978-0-9930099-3-8

Designed by Holywell Press Ltd.
Printed in Great Britain by Holywell Press Ltd., Oxford